Beyond Woofs and Whinnies

Saying that I hear and understand the wise messages from the animal and insect kingdom may be beyond the realm of reality to many. Perhaps this will read more like a science fiction book to those who question this sort of communication. I have also questioned the new and strange information that has come my way, just as you may question the validity of the contents of this book. Yet I have found the more I learn, discern, and experience by looking outside the box in which I live, I realize there is a much bigger world to experience than what I can see with my two eyes and hear with my two ears.

I invite you, the reader, to open your mind and heart as you read my explanations on how I communicated with the animals and the messages they have shared with me. May these messages nurture you on your personal life journey.

When both first and last names are used together in this book, it represents the actual people involved. All others, including some animals' names, have been changed.

Beyond Woofs and Whinnies

Animals understand us better than
we understand ourselves

Karen Wrigley

www.KarenWrigley.com

Book Cover by Artist Revelle Hamilton
Illustrations by Karen Wrigley
Illustrations with quotes and cover picture are available
on various items through my website.

Copyright © 2010 by Karen Wrigley

ISBN 0-7414-5590-0

Book Cover by Artist Revelle Hamilton

Illustrations by Karen Wrigley

Published by:

INFINITY
PUBLISHING.COM

1094 New DeHaven Street, Suite 100
West Conshohocken, PA 19428-2713
Info@buybooksontheweb.com
www.buybooksontheweb.com
Toll-free (877) BUY BOOK
Local Phone (610) 941-9999
Fax (610) 941-9959

Printed in the United States of America

Published January 2010

This book is dedicated to Jake, Sam, Little Joe, Sun Dance, Buster, Jai, Missy, and Xena my four legged friends. Thank you for spending your earthly time with me.

Contents

Listen

A woof and a whinny
Sounds to hear

Yet, listen to the soul
Take note of the heart

Relax thyself
A voice to be heard

It sounds of your own
Yet is not

Offerings of animals
Given with love

Insightful knowledge
Presides

Within
Beyond Woofs and Whinnies

~ Karen Wrigley

Acknowledgments

This is not my book; it belongs to many. I am thankful to everyone who helped—especially, the critter kingdom who expressed their wisdom, needs, and concerns for themselves, their people, and mankind.

My parents, Jim and Edith Page, gave me the gift of living on a farm. My mother understood my need to be with nature. I snuck out the back door many times to be with wild and domestic animals while my sisters worked on household chores. My father taught me to nurture, observe, and appreciate nature. When plowing fields, Dad found baby rabbits whose homes had been unearthed. Gently he tucked them in his big pockets to safely bring them home. My mother provided many eyedroppers for feeding little ones.

My husband John patiently taught me how to have a healthy relationship with my computer. John built my website and catered to many of my needs. His background in sales created opportunities for me as an animal communicator.

My sons, Craig and Kirk Little, supported me with encouraging words, business advice, and creative ideas for promoting this book and myself.

My brother Dan possesses a great wisdom about life. When I visited Dan, his wife Namaste, and her daughter Nayomi in Washington, I communicated with several animals at a nearby nature park. These animals' stories are in this book.

My stepson, Keith Wrigley, a computer wizard, provided the laptop I used to write this book.

My community's Lake Writers was supportive with advice and encouragement. Several literary midwives, mostly from the writers group, helped birth *Beyond Woofs and Whinnies*.

My first midwife, Becky Mushko, an ex-English teacher, and accomplished writer with numerous writing awards, bludgeoned my sentences with her red pen. Her encouraging words brought my writing to a new level. She suggested *Beyond Woofs and Whinnies* for this book's title.

Second midwife, mystery writer Sally Roseveare, continually reminded me of my purpose. As Sally proof-read the chapters, she giggled and cried at the animals' insightful messages.

Third midwife, Kathy Bauch, Senior Director of the Humane Society of the United States, graciously supported me with her input, insight, and contacts. Her encouragement for me to stay true to myself was valuable.

Fourth midwife, Sue Coryell, fine-tuned my writing and helped me stay focused on publishing *Beyond Woofs and Whinnies*.

Fifth midwife, Betsy Ashton, read for details and continuity.

Revelle Hamilton, a talented local artist, created the cover picture.

LeAndra Shepherd photographed the back cover picture. The horse, Maestoso II Griselda IV, barn mane "Griz," a Lipizzaner, belongs to the Smiths at Centerline View Farm.

Ron Gordon enhanced my back book cover photo of Griz and me.

Tiana Hickman, Ginny Brock, Carol Rosen, Ruth Raymond, Pat Hafford, and Wendy Guiffre provided publishing and promotional ideas as well as motivational pushes.

Sue Gordon, Judy Johnson, Lisa Russel, Brenda and Ray Sullivan, Mary Tokarski, and Bret Keister read my book for a test drive before being published. Suggestions and corrections were taken, especially when said, "Get the book published, it's good."

Introduction

"The best and most beautiful things in the world cannot be seen or touched. They must be felt within the heart."

~Helen Keller

Was there one moment in my life when it occurred to me that my understanding of animals was any more acute than anyone else's? No. Understanding animals was a natural part of who I was—who I am. It set me apart from most other people.

My first conscious communication with an animal happened late one evening in my mother's kitchen. I was five years old. Neighbors had brought a new pet, a baby rabbit, to our house to visit. The adults went to another room for a game of cards. The other children went off to play, and I stayed with the baby rabbit. As he hopped around and explored the corners of the kitchen, I knew immediately that he was looking for water. I watched him for a while, but did nothing about it until my mother came into the kitchen for coffee.

"The bunny is thirsty," I said.

"Then give him some water," she answered.

I reached down into the cabinet for a mason jar lid, filled it with water, then watched the bunny drink. And drink. And drink. I don't know how I knew he was thirsty. I just knew.

As a child, I observed people and tried to comprehend their behavior, yet my mind could not understand their ways. People were complicated beings. Animals and their behavior were simple and clear. Animals and nature provided a simple life, a freedom to be me.

"She's different," the girls whispered.

High-pitched giggling usually followed their whispers. I was definitely outside of the circle, and it was hurtful. But I had a secret that I was not about to expose—I knew what they were thinking before they ever put their thoughts into childish words.

At times like these, I climbed bareback upon my pinto pony, Little Joe; a saddle was intrusive. Little Joe was my friend, always there for me. I often loaded up my secrets on Little Joe and lost myself in the safety of the woods. Sometimes I went to the willow tree in the back yard where I could sit with the sound of the wind rustling its branches. I watched a myriad of birds flying free in the wind, their colorful bodies swooping around me. Their singing brought joy to my ears. Perched high in my own pretend nest, I watched the wind swirl the wheat, ruffle the great green corn leaves in surrounding fields, and send the spirit of nature my way.

The cornfield surrounding our home was a special haven teeming with critters. There were snakes, raccoons, rabbits and bunches of bugs. After a rain, night crawlers were everywhere and the luscious mud between my toes grounded me to the earth. On sunny days I loved the feel of sunshine on my freckled skin. I watched filtering rays light the dense forest of cornstalks. My vision—my soul—followed the bright pathways upward to great bursts of glorious white light shining through clouds. It dazzled my eyes, and showed me the way to more than I could understand. This cornfield, planted by my father, is where my budding knowledge was nurtured, cultivated, allowed to grow, and bloomed into an unspoken knowledge which I would learn to share.

Write Our Words

I had been hearing a voice inside my head for several months, "the message is not clear," something about writing a book. I did not want this message to be clear. Please let the message be for someone else! My grammar and spelling skills are at the bottom—no, below bottom—of my talents. I succeeded for months in talking myself out of the idea.

However, the realization finally came. I heard—*Write our words, we have much to share.* The message spoken by the animals vibrated through my being; chills ran down my spine. My blinders were off. I was guided to use simple words, keep the messages understandable to all, and have individual conversations with a variety of critters who wished to share.

A few days later, with a pad of paper and pencil, I began to write.

1

Be True to Whom

"The wind of heaven is that which blows between a horse's ears. The horse is God's gift to mankind."

~Arabian proverb

As I settle into a comfortable chair to prepare for my first communication for this book, my thoughts expand outward to all my animal friends and I give a mental invitation to any one who might have a message.

Perrier, a 23-year-old thoroughbred I have been communicating with, lovingly makes herself known. Her job—or should I say her joy—is described best by her person, Fran Ichjo: "She is an incredible horse, lots of heart and wisdom. She loves to compete, participating in 'eventing'—a competition with three phases: dressage, cross-country, and stadium jumping. She has a huge jump and moves beautifully in dressage. The more active she is, the better she is. She is proud of her youth!"

Perrier is my friend. This is her message:

Get on with it! Set time aside! (She is speaking of my communications for the book.) *I have much direction, finding it powerful, and satisfying. You may not be clear all the time compiling animal communications, yet you are able to accomplish something. Perhaps wavering at times, your heart is in the right place and you will succeed.*

You pledge your allegiance to "Americus." Pledge it to the great being you are and this approach will serve you and Americus, the "Us" of the great land in a grander, more glorious fashion beyond your wildest dreams.

Be careful with whom you share your projects or goals. Hold this tight for now. You are telepathic! Other people's thoughts you may pick up on or their verbal words could cause concerns about validity in your talents and trusting yourself as a communicator as well as a writer. Don't be discouraged if the progression of this project is not what you want it to be. It will all come together.

"I am extremely thankful, Perrier; I will take your advice. I am open for more."

Choose whom you work with wisely. Not all are what they seem; discernment is important.

"Thank you once again. Do you have more to share?"

No, I am quite thorough.

I found this witty, for she is a Thoroughbred.

"Do you have a message for us?"

Indeed, a horse's world can be wonderful; it can be horrible too, like people's. I have been proven to be sound, and good at what I do. I focus on what I like and do the best I can. Because of this, I have been well taken care of. The kind and good spirit that I am has brought the same to me. If you serve and treat others with respect, they will do the same to you.

I have had an excellent life; the reason—I take pleasure in myself and love all that is around me. Live your life fully. Do what brings you satisfaction and joy, honoring others around you on your journey, never letting go of the vision of what you are and are becoming. Bring this way of being to your personal life, job, projects and other aspects of your living. Release what you perceive as obstacles around you, especially those inside of you. Once on to better things, give thanks for the obstacles—for they gave you knowledge of the benefits of conflict, thereby redirecting you on a better path.

Perrier pauses, then asks, *Have I given a clear message?*

"Yes, an inspiring, clear message, thank you."

~~~~~~~~~~~~•••~~~~~~~~~~~~

Engage, Be Brave

I believe everyone has telepathic abilities to different degrees. Humans are born with intuition, extrasensory abilities, gut feelings, knowingness; the list goes on describing an innate ability to "know" without reason. Children use this sense quite naturally early in life. Often, as children grow, they use it less and less and soon it is forgotten. Their natural ways are not cultivated and, in many cases, are discouraged. If adults were to recognize these special gifts within themselves, as well as encourage their children to use them, we would live in a different world. These innate capabilities can help us understand the world with compassion, love and higher knowledge; they give direction and understanding in all aspects of life in ways for a happier, easier, contented life.

There is evidence that, now more than ever, children with empathic, or extrasensory perception are being born. A few names given to these incredible children are: Crystal, Star, and Indigo. These beautiful children put a smile on my face.
~~~~~~~~~~~~

Because this is an animal communication book I will not elaborate and recommend those interested to investigate this subject further through books and searching on the internet.

An article had been written about my animal communications and specifically about an eagle at the lake. Because of this article I received a call from Nancy, a local lady. Her strong love for eagles caused her to call. She was looking for someone, anyone, who believed in spirituality the way she does. She said she had lived in the lake area for six years and had found no one she could share and grow with. I asked her if she had shared what she was looking for with anyone. The answer was no. Well, no wonder. She was shocked to hear two people within a few miles from her home had the same beliefs. She explained she was fearful of what people would think or do if she brought the subject up.

More people than ever in history are open to and are participating in communicating with people and animals who have passed over. They are engaging in animal communication, dowsing, astrology, numerology, and the power of thought. They are exploring crystals, shamans, gurus, channeling angels and evolved beings. Christianity, Buddhism and Judaism are all recognized for their common denominators allowing for differences. TV, radio, and print shout unity. Burning people at the stake and stoning people are now illegal. Speak up! Share with love and understanding towards others and yourselves.

When we moved to Smith Mountain Lake, in the Bible Belt, I met a handful of individuals in a five-day period all wanting to share and learn more of angels, alternative healing, facets of spirituality, and other interests. All of them but one, I had met for the first time. I called them a couple days later and invited them to my home to discuss these subjects. They all came at 9:00 AM and stayed until 4:00 PM. From that day on, for six years we met every Wednesday at my home for a full day. We missed only a couple of days in the six years. Southern Baptist, Catholic, Methodist, Jewish, and Unitarian all sat together. We kept the group to no more than twelve, usually smaller. We eventually started taking turns meeting in each others' homes. As others took on more responsibilities, I backed off.

I am pleased the group continues to meet. From the interest of this one group, now there are other groups meeting in this area. One circle generated several, and I believe there will be more. I am pleased with what came from that one day when a handful of people said, "Yes, I want to know more."

Nancy joined the group and we became friends. Two years later Nancy passed over, and now she soars with the eagles.

As a child, and young adult, I did not share my intuition or telepathic abilities. Now I believe it is most important to share my experiences. I have been in the presence of others who are fearful of an experience they have had. A sweet lady actually thought her children would put her in an insane asylum for seeing her husband at her bed side after he passed. For her to know it was a gift, not a curse, brought great relief. A child shared with her mother what their golden retriever was telling her. The mother was relieved to hear her daughter was not crazy. I am hopeful my experiences will encourage others to feel safe and comfortable and enable them to share their experiences and abilities with others, as well.

2

Angel in My Life

"Bread may feed my body but my horse feeds my soul."

~Author Unknown

Jake was an out-of-the-ordinary horse. His presence supported and changed my life.

My first husband gave me a young and beautiful black half-Arabian horse for my birthday, but keeping this spirited, untrained horse was out of the question because our one and a half year old son, Craig, would be with me around this horse. As disappointed as my husband was to give up the half-Arabian, we came across another horse—Jake, a five-year-old, buckskin. He was not a showy horse like the

Arabian. What showed on Jake were his ribs and a dull coat. But Jake had something inside him the Arabian did not—a gentle personality with a large heart that fit me just fine. It was love at first sight! I knew that with tender loving care and good feed, Jake could be a healthy, happy horse. My husband was not pleased with my decision, yet Jake would prove to be a Godsend.

This special horse took great care to act in a safe manner whenever Craig was near. Craig took his naps on Jake while we rode on nearby trails. We could ride down the middle of a four-lane highway with semi-trailers screaming on both sides and Jake would never flinch. At times when Jake was grazing, Craig would walk up to him and wrap his arms around the horse's large head. Jake would stop eating, keep his head low and love his hug as much as Craig. They stood perfectly still until they both had their fill. One of Craig's favorite places was under Jake's belly where he would play or simply sit. A special haven, he felt safe and enjoyed knowing this space was just for him. It seemed to be a sacred place for Craig. Perhaps it was.

During an accident Jake and I had, I realized even more what a precious gift this horse was. Jake and I were returning to the barn after a brisk ride in early autumn. Just before we turned a corner into a wooded area, I checked my watch. I needed to be home in time to make dinner for company. My next memory was waking up next to a large muddy area with an excruciating headache that rendered me helpless. I struggled several times, prying myself off the ground but always crumbling back down in agony. The pain—more than I could manage—was compounded with a dizzy, nauseous feeling. I then realized Jake was standing next to me, his side muddy like mine. We had fallen while turning a corner in a shady area which hid a patch of mud.

My body parts moved as they should. I was thankful I had no broken bones. I managed to grab the stirrup and, using all my strength, pulled myself up on to Jake. My loving friend did all he could to help me by standing perfectly still and staying as close as possible to me.

Checking my watch, I realized I had been unconscious for ten minutes, and Jake, evidently, had stood by me the whole time. After I managed to pull myself into the saddle, my body drooped over his neck, and my feet dangled along his sides. Jake slowly, gently carried me back to the barn. I depended on this horse like I had never before depended on anyone in my life.

Once off Jake, I blocked as much pain as possible from my mind. I needed to unsaddle Jake and check him for injuries, but then realized I could not see peripherally from my left eye. I remember a sense of Jake telling me he was fine and to take care of myself. Close to collapsing, I ignored him and quickly looked over his body and observed how he moved his body. Jake—thank goodness—was okay, and now I needed to act on Jake's advice.

Fortunately, I lived only a few miles away. In a state of shock, I drove myself home. Once in the house, I allowed myself to relax—and then my life became more frightening yet. My mind seemed to stop functioning. I could not remember who was coming for dinner or what I was to prepare. I was nauseous, my body hurt and felt as if my head would explode. I vaguely remember my parents arriving to watch Craig, and my husband driving me to the hospital.

After a day in the hospital, my sight and memory improved. I was discharged and directed to a specialist for my head injury. Sitting in front of the specialist I found it strange that he asked me to stick my tongue out at him. Stranger yet, it veered slightly to the right. Because of my tongue's behavior, the doctor wanted me to schedule a follow-up test. I wrinkled my forehead, tipped my head slightly and ignored his advice. I could not be bothered with a cockeyed tongue and claimed it would get better, as would my head pain. Fortunately, both did but it took a few months before I was back to my usual feisty self. As for my brain damage—that depends on who you talk to!

Shortly after the accident, I discovered I was pregnant with our second son, Kirk.

Trusting this horse completely, I rode many times during my pregnancy with Craig in the saddle with me. I learned from Jake to be more careful, to believe in him if he gave me a cue not to head into a particular area or showed any signs of concern.

After my second son's birth, we moved Jake to my parents' farm, a considerable distance away. With a new baby and the distance between us, I missed my dear Jake. I soon faced the difficult realization that I must sell him. My husband, a military man, had received orders to a new location. If that wasn't bad enough, I had been having recurring dreams of turning a corner and seeing Jake lying lifeless on the ground.

Before I could sell Jake, an upsetting phone call came from my mother. Jake was in their barn lot and would not get up. The vet had examined him, but could find nothing wrong. I bundled up the kids and headed out to Jake. Leaving Kirk with my mother, I took Craig with me to the barn where Jake was. The same feeling came over me as in the dream. Fearing the worst, I told Craig to sit and wait for me on top of a hill close to the barn where I could see him but he could not see Jake. As I walked to the barn my whole body constricted, a lump filled my throat, my legs grew weak. I fearfully, slowly, with a heavy heart stepped around the corner of my parents' barn where Jake was. I felt I was walking into my nightmare. I had no choice.

My nightmare was now reality. Jake's body, laid lifeless on the ground.

Because animal communication is done through thought, and there is life after death, one can animal communicate with a loved one in body the same as when the spirit has left the body. It has been a long time since I have been in touch with Jake. I am apprehensive for I never resolved Jake's passing or felt closure. My hurried, to-do list of preparing for a move and being a mother for my two young boys gave me no time to grieve or understand what caused Jake's death.

I connect with Jake.

When I communicate with an animal out of body, the sensations or vibrations are lighter, less dense. I hear, *I am in the beyond, beyond, a place of only love. Don't fret over past experiences wishing you could change circumstances; they were learning and loving times for both of us. My time had come to move on, as it was for you to move.*

Have you made the most of your life?

I answered Jake. I did not hold true to creating a happy life early on, but now I know to use personal discernment in making decisions, not take life so serious, enjoy the small things, appreciate more, and laugh as much as possible.

"I have regrets, mostly of going through the same problem over and over again till I finally get the lesson, even if it causes brain damage!"

Jake enjoys my sense of humor! He continues, *Being aware of what is around you, even if you cannot see it, affects your life, like mud puddles. Who knows what is around the corner when your two eyes do not see. Be aware with your "know that you know that you know" or the old words, sixth sense, and you won't get dirty or brain damage!*

I came to you giving joy and love during difficult times, and to set an example that when your mission is done, it is time to leave for another. My earthly tasks have been accomplished and now I am in bliss, or as some may prefer, heaven. During your meditations I have come many times as a large winged white horse to help. You know, you remember me. I now serve you in a different realm. I do it unwaveringly as I carried you and your family before.

Loved one, live your life to the fullest. Enjoy your journey. I am there when you call.

"From my heart I thank you, Jake. It has been over twenty-five years since we were together. The memories are special, yet I know I have forgotten many."

All that matters is the love I gave, and the love you gave back, which you remember well, and what that can do for you and those you walk with. This is what is important.

"I am thankful you were in my corner. Even corners seem different now! Do you have wisdom to share for others?

There are special times coming. Purge yourselves of old habits, thoughts, and health problems, which no longer serve you. Make way for a cleaner Earth, in all aspects. This will make your walk of life much easier. Simply carry out your purpose, your joy on this planet. There is another corner to turn. Rejoice, good times are ahead, no matter how dismal things may seem.

"You came to my thoughts and I did not answer. My mind was filled with the 'what ifs'—what if I checked on you earlier, what if I took better care of you, what if I did and you had lived. You helped me once again. You helped me purge, as you called it. I quit beating myself up and released the pain surrounding your death. I now have peace."

As I reread Jake's message I remember how I soften corners in my home by setting a basket, or plant in front of them. I want the corners I turn to be pleasant, not only in my home, but in my life. A corner is an angle, a word close to the word angel. I wonder, are the two related? The corner Jake speaks of in his message is for all of us. I believe angels and other enlightened beings are helping with change on this planet and their help will make turning our corners easier, perhaps beautiful. It is up to you and me; it is a choice we make.

~~~~~~~~~~~~••~~~~~~~~~~~~

Feelings into Words

When I am receiving a feeling, an awareness, or knowingness, at times I have to dig deep into my brain to find the most accurate words to describe what I am receiving. As I select my words, I heighten my sensitivity to
~~~~~~~~~~~~

the words' vibrations and compare the vibrations to the information given me by the animal. The better it feels comparing the two, the more correct my information is for the animal's person.

For example, I once was communicating with a little white pony who said he was "scared" about his person going on vacation. But I realized after I said the word "scared," my feelings or sensitivity to the word did not fit or feel comfortable with the feelings I received from the animal. I then used the word "concerned," which resonated much better with the feeling I received. The pony was "concerned" about who would take care of him while his person was on vacation. The word "concerned" is more gentle than "scared." The word scared, upset the pony's person. I should have discerned the word more carefully before speaking. After sharing the correct word, the pony's person was able to ease his mind by giving details how he would be taken care of.

3

I, Like the Buddha

"All knowledge, the totality of all questions and all answers, is contained in the dog."

~Franz Kafka

I had no classes or books to teach me how to understand what the animals wanted to say, and I wanted to find out if how I was communicating was similar to those who called themselves "animal communicators." I decided to attend an animal communication class. During the class, I was introduced to Loreli, a long-haired miniature dachshund, who lived with June Hughes, also known as Sananjaleen.

Once class started, Loreli, "the ringleader," directed the class through Sananjaleen. If the class got sidetracked to another subject, Loreli would meander out of the room. Once class got back on track, she would reappear.

During the class, our instructor gave us a postcard with a picture of Loreli and a statue of Buddha that she had taken in her flower garden. Loreli wanted the animal communicators to know she was like the Buddha. My mind tried to make sense of this. How could a dog be like the Buddha? Shortly after June gave this message to the class, Loreli walked toward where I was sitting on the floor with the postcard in front of me. Loreli glanced up, looked deep into my eyes, and quickly put her little black nose on the postcard and held it there for half a second. She glanced back up, again looking deep into my eyes, and said, *That is I, like the Buddha. I know you doubt.* And she walked away.

That day created a whole new world for me about the possibilities within the animal kingdom.

Several weeks later, I spoke to a reporter who lived in Washington, D.C. I explained how profoundly this little dog had influenced me. Being a curious reporter, she asked if she could attend a class. I mentioned that perhaps Loreli would repeat her "Buddha and I" message for us. The reporter attended the next class with me. Once again, I put Loreli's picture on the floor. Mentally, I told her why we were there, the possibilities it could bring with a reporter present, and asked if she would point herself out again on the postcard. Loreli was not in sight as I was sending the message to her telepathically, for it was one of those times when the class had wandered off course. Shortly afterwards she showed herself, walked across the room straight to the postcard, whisked her nose close to her face on the postcard, looked up at us, and walked away, as if to say, "Do I have to prove myself again?" We could hardly believe our eyes!

As Loreli and I kept close in our communications, I later discovered she had orchestrated my first day with her. Perhaps it would take one like the Buddha to accomplish a day like this and the ones that followed. Because of my experience with Loreli and my reporter friend, I was given many opportunities to inform and share experiences with believers and non-believers in fun and interesting ways. For example, in a posh downtown D.C. hotel, I attended a puppy shower complete with hors d'oeuvres in the shape of dog bones. The new pup received presents from both human and canine guests.

My most interesting engagement when living in Northern Virginia, however, was attending the Bark Ball at Loews L'Enfant Plaza Hotel in D.C. This elaborate affair supports the Washington, D.C. Humane Society/SPCA. People and dogs came to the event dressed in formal attire. Some canines in attendance: a poodle in a long shiny pink gown, her head adorned with tiara matching her person's costume; a boxer proudly showing off his fancy tux; and a few barking, saying they would rather be running in their back yards and *not* wearing a silly outfit. A doggy bar with Evian water and kibbles was elegantly presented on the floor while their human companions dined on hor d'oeuvres and wine served on stylishly decorated tables. When all had partaken of food and drink, both two and four-legged guests danced on a beautifully decorated ballroom floor. As people boogied down on the dance floor, dog companions pranced around their people with little hops and barks.

I did not have time to learn how to handle the media explosion that followed. I had some challenging times as I dealt with reporters and radio interviewers. I was not accustomed to talking live on radio shows with thousands of people listening. Writers for newspapers and magazines were usually honest, yet at times twisted my words. I was told by a friend in the media that a new subject or interest in D.C. is usually worn hard, and then forgotten. I could see the fast-moving pace of my newfound career was slowing down in the D.C area and wondered if I should breathe new life into my profession at home, or if my journey would take me elsewhere.

Through a series of events, my husband and I moved south to live on Smith Mountain Lake in Virginia. From our home, I received calls for communications from around the United States and other countries. Animal communication is my joy. I drop the "b" in job and add a "y." It is my joy, not my job.

I asked Loreli if she was pleased with what I had written. She said, *Yes, be clear, ordain them into this new world they are about to discover and help them to know we are part of God, too.*

~~~~~~~~~~~~~••~~~~~~~~~~~~~

Whose Thought Is It?

There is a subtle difference between the animal's thoughts that come to me versus my own thoughts. When hearing words from an animal, I hear my own voice, but the emotions and energy are different from mine.

When I receive information from animals, the right side of my brain—the intuitive side—seems to be more dominant. When I translate or analyze, the left side of my brain—the analytical side—is engaged.

While discussing the difference between the left and right side of the brain with my client Patsy, her dog Maggie abruptly interrupted me. Maggie most intently expressed herself: *Do a reality check in your space of mind. Use the mind as a whole.* When information comes this clearly, it is important. I no longer speak of the left and right side of the brain as being separate. I realize they work together, as one.
~~~~~~~~~~~~~

4

Seek the Unseen

"Man can no longer live for himself alone. We must realize that all life is valuable and that we are united to all life. From this knowledge comes our spiritual relationship to the universe."

~ Author Unknown

Tiggy, a long-haired red dachshund, has been my teacher for several years. I first met this sweet-natured girl at June Hughes' house when I inquired about other animal communicators. Tiggy is one of the reasons I am writing this book. Her wisdom has changed my life. Tiggy was an elderly lady when I met her. Her muzzle was quite grayed, and she moved rather slowly, yet her spirit was lively.

Late one night, I felt Tiggy's presence in my mind. At that time, pre-Smith Mountain Lake, one of my favorite spots was relaxing in a steam bath in the complex where my husband and I lived in Northern Virginia. Hot moisture relaxed my muscles, and sweat poured off my body, Tiggy spoke to me gently. She said she would teach me many things about myself and the world if I were to meet her mentally in the sauna each Wednesday night around 10:00 PM.—and so I did. The sauna supported a healthier body for me as Tiggy supported a healthier mind and spirit. With pen and paper ready, once a week for a month I had a date with Tiggy. She asked me questions and I had to look for answers within myself. For example, she asked, what was important to me? I wrote many pages until I could go no further. My writing and thinking came to one word—joy. Tiggy then gave me some sage advice: *Love yourself and others and be in joy or peace no matter what is going on around you physically or in your mind.* Tiggy said to always look into another's eyes with love. I asked her, "What if I cannot?" Her reply: *Look away.*

Twelve years later I have to remind myself of these words. Tiggy's advice is getting easier to follow and has been worth the effort.

When I committed to the animal kingdom, and they asked me to be their voice, Tiggy came to my mind telepathically, for one of my first communications:

Once man found the Earth was not flat....It took courage to find this route of knowingness and adventure. What brought it forth in them—a restlessness—there was more than what met the eye. And now....what is there more than the visual eye? Angels, souls who have left their bodies, nature beings—so much more you do not see. Many people are showing those that cannot "see" or "hear" that there is more in this world of greatness for them. These people showing the way are bold and confident in this truth.

You see far, far less than what there truly is. The ratio of what there is you don't see to what you do see is one trillion to one.

Go adventure, seek the unseen, the journey will bring great Joy and Love.
I Am
Tiggy

~~~~~~~~~~~~•••~~~~~~~~~~~~

Wrong or Right Animal

At times, when focusing on an animal intended for a communication, a different animal unaccountably makes himself known. For example, when several animals are living together, the more dominant animal in the household may step up to be the spokes-animal. On occasion, a deceased animal will seize the moment to express a needed message, usually pertaining to information and guidance to resolve personal issues and sad or regretful feelings about his death. More recently, animals that I and my client do not know have boldly come through with precise remarkable information pertaining to the purpose of the communication.

Once I described a dog making himself known to my client, Pam. She was certain he was not her dog. I refocused on her mixed-breed dog, Buddy. Further into the communication, Pam gasped. She suddenly realized the mystery dog was Mick, a border collie who had escaped from her back yard several years ago. He showed me that he now had a fenced-in back yard and children to play with. Life was good. Mick wanted to thank Pam for the care she gave him and to let her know what had happened to him. Pam's lingering worries were resolved.

I have learned that sometimes the "wrong" animal making himself known, is the "right" animal for that moment.

Often when I communicate with an animal that has passed, I find my attention diverted to a person or another
~~~~~~~~~~~~

animal on the other side that is with the departed animal. This person or animal is usually close to my client. My client is comforted knowing Spot is with Uncle Bob or Daisy—two beings they love are with each other. As I share messages from the other side—Grandmother, child, friend, dog, cat, or horse—I can sense my client feeling better by the minute.

A long-haired white cat unexpectedly made herself known to me during a communication with my client's recently passed dog. I discovered this cat was my client's cat ten years ago. The cat then brought my mind to an older lady. I described her to my client. My client asked what her name was. I heard, Anny or Annabel. My client said one name was her grandmother's name; the other was her husband's grandmother's name. Hearing both names surprised me because receiving names is not one of my strengths. I now knew I had tapped into a party on the other side. Both grandmothers let me know there were others with them and all were in an extraordinarily good place. Both grandmothers took turns eagerly sharing their love and pride for my client's family and imparting bits of information to support them in their walk of life.

When communications take place such as this one, my clients receive a nice surprise with added benefits.

5

Out of Balance

"I have studied many philosophers and many cats. The wisdom of cats is infinitely superior."

~Hippolyte Taine

Max is an Ocicat, a large long-legged cat hybrid, created by combining the Abyssinian and Siamese cat. This breed's behavior is much like that of a dog. An Ocicat is like a puppy, eager to please and willing to play retrieving games. Ocicats will walk with a leash and respond to training. They need ample exercise, so safe access to the outdoors is essential.

I had a communication with Max earlier in the week. He had been dealing with three problems: house renovations, a new puppy and new housing construction around his home. His freedom to roam outside was severely limited, and these stresses had caused him to take on the swell of emotions within his household. His immune system had been weakened and he was now ill.

My thoughts are directed to Max to see how he is doing.

I am doing much better. I am fortunate, I have a family doing all they can to help me through these times. I can tell you are not well, Karen. Your health will get better. Your stress and mine have caused us to let situations around us affect our well-being.

What Max said was true; I was not feeling well!

"I am usually aware of my environment, and how I react to it makes a difference whether I stay in balance or not. In this case . . . not!"

Life is filled with many learning situations.

"You're familiar with my collection of animals' messages to humans. Would you like to contribute?" I asked.

Not feeling well, it might be difficult for you to be receptive, so to speak. When one does not feel well, it is time to do something about it. You and I had an earlier private conversation about seeing the signs and acting on what needs to be done. I think this is one of them, Karen.

"Max, what should I do?"

This is something everyone needs to discern for themselves. Our bodies tell us what we need more than some doctors. We forgot how to listen to our bodies and respect what they say. Sometimes our body tells us we need a doctor! Do you?

"My chiropractor adjusted my back today. In retrospect, I could have put a warm compress on my muscles and rested to manage my needs. As I think about it, the chiropractor said I should do this as well."

That's what I'm talking about. You were out of balance, so you made an out-of-balance decision. This is when we need to pay extra attention to what is going on, and it is usually the most difficult time to do so. It's a great lesson. Odd as it may sound, it can be interesting and enjoyable. This can be applied to other aspects of life as well: let go of past conditioning and let the answers come.

"I shall take your advice, Max. Why do you have your illness when you seem so wise?"

House animals are in humans' control. I know I need to be outside even more now. Yet my persons don't trust the outside circumstances where greater dangers lurk. My tendency of taking on stress as I deal with my surroundings and people are situations I need to manage better.

I personally think too much has taken place here.

I am pleased to say my companions called an animal communicator to see what I believed would help me and are looking into alternative health care. They are working on all aspects of my life: physical, mental and spiritual. As you mentioned once to me, a mental adjustment, or how we view our circumstances, can be changed.

"I can change my circumstance. On that note, I will put a warm compress on my neck muscles, curl up with a good book, and enjoy. Thanks, Max, for helping me remember. What are you going to do?"

I am going to sit on my cat perch in front of our window and know busy people are coming home from work. They are probably more stressed than I. I'll not forget how lucky I am to be loved and know my people are doing everything they can to keep me healthy. When I do go outside, I will participate with the outside in a fuller manner, soaking up all I can, and when I come back inside, I'll bring it in with me!

You are appreciated Max, may your message open people's eyes to the needs of their animal companions and to themselves.

~~~~~~~~~~~~•••~~~~~~~~~~~

Dismiss Nothing

I have learned not to dismiss any thought that comes to my mind, no matter how ridiculous the thought seems. After I asked a black Labrador Retriever if there were any special foods he would like to eat, I saw a watermelon and an ice cube in my mind. The dog's person laughed out loud and explained the dog loves frozen watermelon. She had given him this treat in past summers, and with hot weather approaching—well, her lab had not forgotten.

An experience during a communication I had helped me to understand a sick cat. I immediately saw in my mind an advertisement I had seen on TV depicting a stomach with an antacid medicine slowly coating the stomach lining. In order to understand the energy essence of what the cat was sending, my brain went through its memory banks so I could relate to the problem. If I receive information that is related to my own personal experience, that information comes so I may understand what the animal is trying to convey. Never disregard any form of information, it comes in many ways. The cat had an upset stomach.
~~~~~~~~~~~~

6

Fishing for Emotions

"But ask now the beasts, and they will teach thee; and the fowls of the air, and they shall tell thee: Or speak to the earth, and it shall teach thee: and the fishes of the sea shall declare unto thee."

~Job 12: 7-**8**

My husband, John, and I enjoy feeding a variety of fish at our Smith Mountain Lake pier. Carp, a bold, scavenger fish, are notorious for congregating whenever food is offered. They, along with the usual catfish, sunfish, baitfish and other finned friends, come swimming when they sense we are approaching the pier.

Buford is a large-mouth bass. Buford knows he has plenty to eat at our pier. When we scatter purchased fish food or whole grain bread over the water, usually twice a day, a multitude of frenzied fish dart out of hiding for a tasty snack. This gives Buford a meal ticket, fine dining on little fish.

Though John and I have seen many bass come and go from our pier, Buford was different. Whenever John or I stood on the pier, he would surface to water's edge; bob up and down with the waves, as he watched our every move with his large dark eyes. I will never forget the day Buford swam next to me as I walked to the end of our pier. Dogs, cats, and horses have followed me, and now wild fish! Buford was a bit picky about showing himself to others, for he made himself known only when John and I were on the pier. It was easy to recognize Buford; he was one and a half feet long, the longest bass at our pier.

Once, this same large bass came a few inches from my hand while I was hand-feeding other fish. I instinctively reached out to pet him. I could not believe he let me stroke part of his long smooth side. Bass can move extremely fast. My mind stopped for a moment; surely it must have been a fluke, I thought as I pulled my hand out of the water. Within seconds, my mind trying to make sense of this bass's actions, I quickly lowered my hand back into the water. He circled back; I held my hand open. As he moved towards me, I gently moved my hand towards him. Time stopped. Just behind his head his body touched the side of my hand. He turned, positioning his body to touch the inside of my hand. I watched and felt this long fish press the full length of his body against my hand. I watched and felt this fish moving as if in slow motion past the palm of my hand—when in reality it had to have been a second or two. I pulled my hand out of the water and jumped up in amazement. My voice shot up an octave as I shared my miraculous moment with John. He made the comment that he was used to things like this happening around me. But I will never get used to it. Each experience is different and incredibly special.

I was now endeared to Buford.

When an animal makes himself known like Buford did, I know another chapter to *Beyond Woofs and Whinnies* is about to take place.

As I sway in our hammock at the water's edge, my laptop ready for Buford's comments, I ask him to present himself. I have a difficult time finding him in thought, then suddenly I see him in front of me in my mind, very close, face-to-face, and larger than life. He is as bold in this amorphous state as he is in the water. His energy is different from that of four-legged critters. It seems light and airy, yet ironically powerful. As I continue to focus in on him, he has the presence of a "wise one."

I am on pins and needles to see what knowledge Buford will share with us. I soon discover Buford is also a "wise guy."

Buford begins:

We know a lot more than you think. Just because we live in the water doesn't mean I don't have a brain. Please don't start comparing size! You don't have the grace we have in the water; you're rather awkward at times. Perhaps you should practice moving in tune with the land as we move in tune with the water and birds with the air.

We know when you are coming to the pier by the vibrations in the land when you walk; the water then emphasizes the vibration even more. Your walk to the pier is the dinner bell for the resident fish. Vibration is very important. People have forgotten its importance. Some think they are sensitive to vibration, their surroundings and emotions. That's a laugh—or should I say gill waving! Now, there is a subject to talk about.

Emotions, what are they? Fear, hate, sadness, anger are crutches people carry around and use for excuses. Emotions are meant to serve, if used appropriately, not control you. Emotions are a tool to learn from, with situations past or present. Once you figure out what caused the emotion, use that brain of yours, so much bigger than ours, and take action on what you have learned regarding the cause of the emotion. Do not waste your energy from emotions that drain you—learn, grow from them. We do not carry emotions the same as you folks, so I will give an example you might relate to. How does this fish know so much? I won't go overboard. Did you like my clever wordage? I know so much more than most of you! So I will keep it simple.

Buford begins his example:

A young boy is living in a busy household and he feels left out. Mom and Dad each have jobs, plus they are constantly keeping up with house and yard work, laundry and life, as people have created it. Young Benny, their son, is not getting the attention he needs. His behavior turns him into a whimpering, annoying, little brat. Now Mom and Dad can spank him, put him in his room, or throw him in the lake with us fish. We fish do not want him, either.

Mom and Dad had better come up with something that works. What works is for Mom and Dad to start having emotions about little Benny—perhaps, confusion, anger, or annoyance. They may feel like jumping in the lake to get away from little Benny, but we don't want them, either! Mom and Dad should take a look at what is taking place, being adults—at least I hope they are—and look at what is happening within themselves as well as little Benny. They finally realize after little Benny has had several tantrums that there was a real problem, and the problem is not the child "they" brought into the world—the real problem started with them, the parents.

Time to take a look at the whole picture. I bet you would like to jump in the lake about now! Basically, many humans are having the same problem; they have forgotten to love and nurture themselves first, not the laundry or dirty carpet. Once they do this, it will be much easier taking care of responsibilities. This is when we realize some of the responsibilities we have created are not important. What can one get rid of in life that does not serve or bring joy to our life? It's time to be in control of life. Little Benny needs to learn the lesson early in life that love is more important than things. Mom and Dad should set the example by nurturing themselves and little Benny, too. Case closed!

Now if everyone is in a good mood, you may all jump in the lake.

"Thank you for your wise advice, Buford."

On the day of our communication I had seen Buford at the pier. It was the last time I saw him looking at me with his big eyes, bobbing at waters edge. His point was made.

~~~~~~~~~~~~•••~~~~~~~~~~~~

They Hurt, I Hurt

When an animal has a physical pain or ailment and I need to understand more fully what the problem is, I focus on the animal's body with intent to feel what she is feeling. My body then becomes sensitive to the pain or discomfort the animal is experiencing, similar to sympathy pains. Sometimes I imagine I am in the animal's body, as if I *am* the animal, feeling what her body is feeling. I can actually experience, to different degrees, what a dog feels when his feet touch wet grass or his pain when his aching joints hurt.

Here is an example: A dog was limping and his people asked me if I could locate the problem and what had caused it. I automatically felt pain in the muscle on the inside of my right front upper arm. My right arm represents the dog's right front leg. This was not a broken bone or damaged tendon; the tissue feels soft and fleshy. The location where I felt the pain must be a muscle. The dog's owner validates that the dog limps on his front right leg. The dog told me he had been playing on wet large rocks near water when his leg slid out from under him as he ran down a boulder. His people confirm there are large rocks by a creek on their property, just as their dog described. The pain I experience helps me communicate the problem from the dog to his persons.

Relating to an injured animal can be complex. When an animal has a health problem, my mind may be drawn first to
~~~~~~~~~~~~

the animal's body part compensating for the problem, rather than the problem itself. For example: a dog with arthritis in his hips knows his people are aware of the pain in his hips. They are not aware he has been putting more weight on the front of his body to support his back hips. I will feel pain in my neck and head, and my arms which represent his front legs are sore and tired. His body is out of balance from compensating for the extra weight. The animal wants his person to know about the unobvious. I then focus on the injured part to better understand the total problem.

Animals usually have opinions as to how they want to handle their own pain or injury. However, with the best intentions, the animal's people usually decide on a course of treatment they think is best. In the case of the dog hurt while playing on wet rocks, I conveyed the dog's wish to heal on his own to the owners, and that is how they proceeded.

7

Troubled

"Not to hurt our humble brethren is our first duty to them, but to stop there is not enough. We have a higher mission—to be of service to them where ever they require it."

~St. Francis of Assisi

On a clear summer day, my husband John, a friend Rhonda, and her daughter Hannah, Hannah's cousin Jordan, and I journeyed to pick blueberries at TLC orchard in Moneta, Virginia. This organic blueberry orchard also pastures emus. Emus are birds that are similar to, yet smaller than, the ostrich. They stand more than five feet tall and can weigh more than a hundred pounds. The emu's long legs provide speed up to thirty miles per hour. These prehistoric, flightless birds are skittish and curious, and they exhibit odd behavior when in stressful situations. For example, an emu will run into a low wall and keep banging into it until he accidentally turns in another direction. For me, the emus were as much of a draw as the blueberries.

After we parked our car at the orchard, we headed down a little dirt lane. All five of us were happy to be in "picking clothes" and ready to fill our buckets with tasty blueberries. Before entering the blueberry patch, Peg, the owner, announced it was time to feed the emus and asked if we would like to go with her. This was the second time I had met the emu called Friendly Fred. Fred is actually a she, but the name stuck after the difference was discovered. The last time I visited, Fred allowed me to pet and hug her. I hoped she would be as friendly with my friends.

Upon meeting the emus, Friendly Fred approached me and curled her head and long neck against my neck and cheek, a behavior unheard of for an emu. No, she was not soft and cuddly like a dog or cat, her feathers were coarse, yet just as special. Observing Fred's special action, Hannah and Jordan moved closer to hand-feed and pet Fred. Both were naturally comfortable in the presence of these unusual birds.

At the end of our visit, the emu escape artist, Trouble, so named because she somehow gets out of the fence to investigate people, animals, cars, and any changes in and around the blueberry patch, making it her business. Not everyone is comfortable having a large, dark-eyed, big-footed, curious bird in close proximity. It is also a most troublesome ordeal getting her back into her pen. Trouble at this time was roaming the grounds freely when she decided she wanted food. This was a good thing, for Trouble was heading to a pan of emu pellets not far from the entrance to her pen. Peg hoped to coax her a little further into a small

fenced-in area where the entrance to her larger living area was located.

On our first try at gently encouraging Trouble towards the gate, she allowed me to pet her. Such behavior was not normal for this particular emu. I thought her actions were an indication she trusted me. When more people came to help, she panicked and turned in the opposite direction from the gate. We tried several times to herd her back. This was a mistake. Emus do not herd well; they usually follow. Peg enjoys sharing stories of Trouble running beside her golf cart as she drives down her lane to the blueberry patch. Unfortunately, there was no room for a golf cart in this case.

Something came over me; I was becoming frustrated and impatient. I did not use my communication skills to understand Trouble; I was using force. I felt I had to get this emu in the pen! Trouble was now getting more upset and more determined that our direction was not her direction. I should have backed off but persisted until she had finally had enough. She turned and ran into a wire stretched across the ground where blackberries once grew. I watched her fall. She immediately jumped up and limped slightly on her left leg. I was now feeling extra bad and immediately asked Trouble if she was hurt. She replied ever so nicely, *Not to worry, I am fine.*

I realized this accident was my fault. All day this "troubled" me; I couldn't understand my actions, of trying to force Trouble into her pen, and why I hadn't consulted her on how to help solve this situation. I was upset with my behavior. How could I, the animal communicator, do something like this? I decided to make amends. I telepathically connected with Trouble.

"Hello, Trouble, I am sorry I was not thoughtful of your needs. Our situation today brings me back to my belief that I communicate better over the phone than when the animal is physically with me."

Not true, you knew what was going on; something else kicked in—you being hard-headed. I kept trying to tell you I did not want to be trapped in the area that leads to the gate with all those people. I know you heard me say "Open the gate before you guide me into this area," because you asked the children to open the gate as I projected to you what I needed. They could not open it; you should have. It was then that you knew I was not going to do what you wanted. Why did you keep pressing me when it was not working?

"The need to help, not give up."

Just who do you think you were helping?

"You, who needed to be in the safety of your pen; Peg, who was upset you were out of your pen; and the two children, who enjoyed your company and the adventure of guiding you into your pen. I also remember how you let me pet you. I thought you understood I was trying to keep you out of 'trouble.'"

You were focused on one thing; an old behavior kicked in. We have very powerful legs and this is a powerful message. Man over animal. You still have some inside of you, and you do not want to admit it! Man and animal can work together, even with emus. You understand our ways. You enjoyed our physical contact. Fred and I were happy to be close to you. We gave to you, I needed you to give of who you are to me when I was frightened.

"It's difficult for me to believe what you say is true. I don't want to admit that! I don't understand. I have amazing, wonderful experiences around animals. It's special, I cannot explain, it just happens. I thought this was going to be one of those times. It ended up totally wrong.

"I need to take a close look at myself. You seem to know more about this than I, oh wise one. Speak. Enlighten me!"

Don't get cute with me; this goes deeper than you want to admit. You are the one who said during a radio interview that emus were one of the dumbest animals you had met.

"Oh dear, I know animals are psychic, but I was hoping you weren't aware of that incident. I want to put my head in a hole. I apologize. It was my first interview ever and it happened to be the largest radio talk show in the Washington, D.C. area. I was shaking in my boots. I had just visited an emu farm a few days before, and that is how the owners described emus. I realize my irresponsible words have been heavy on my shoulders, and my shoulders just got heavier. Thank you for being aware of my burden and bringing it to the surface. Help."

Be more aware of yourself. Take note of your actions. When they feel uncomfortable, stop, see what is going on inside and around you. In both instances you were uncomfortable in different ways. You were not in your balance and place of peace; I felt this in your presence. That is what triggered me to be even more upset. You are fine-tuning your awareness to help you on your journey.

"So this was a lesson, and you were the teacher?"

Yes, you have been drawn to this orchard for over a year, but we were patient. Some people carry baggage all their lives; it took you five years. Do you feel better?

"Like a boulder off my shoulders. I did not want my words to hurt the emus, yet my words were broadcast to thousands of listeners. I was afraid my harsh words might come back to 'kick' me someday. The collective thoughts of people affect us all. This was freeing. I can't thank you enough. I will be more conscious of what I say and do by being in balance with my emotions and surroundings. I will speak *my truth*, not what other people believe. I hope my lesson will teach others."

Shortly after my communication with Trouble, I was in a conversation with Friendly Fred. She wanted to give Trouble a new name—Busy Bee. Fred explained to me that Trouble was misunderstood. Her intentions are to check out all the activities at TLC and watch over the property. Her "troubles" have turned into her assets, an emu watch dog! Busy Bee is also the official greeter to all that come to pick berries. Later that summer, I told Busy Bee my son Kirk was coming to see her and to pick berries, and if she would please take care of him. And she did. Busy Bee not only followed Kirk the entire time, she told us to follow her to the biggest sweetest berries growing in the patch. And they were.

Busy Bee, we love you.

~~~~~~~~~~~~•••~~~~~~~~~~~~

Lost Animals

My sense of smell came in handy for a lost Jack Russell terrier. When the front door to this terrier's home was left open, he took advantage of the opportunity and ran out the door in need of exercise and adventure. There were several similar parks in this neighborhood, but he showed me how the one he was in was different from the rest. He gave me information I saw in my minds' eye: the faint look of cinder blocks that were square, stacked on top of each other. I could see the light color and texture of cement under his feet. I don't usually pick up on smells as strongly as my other senses, yet I smelled sewage and the odor was strong. Through smell, he showed me what a park bathroom smells like after a full day of use on a hot, humid day! A poor sniffer could not get this one wrong! Only one park in the area had a restroom. The dog's person knew where that park was, yet the dog was not there when the person arrived. He had moved on because he was having a good time and was not ready to be in an enclosed area—called home—as he conveyed in the communication. He wanted to roam, and roam he did, for another full day. When he'd had his fill of the great outdoors, he let a kind person catch him. Because he had an identification tag, he was returned home. There was no confirmation this little dog was in the park about which I had received information. When the dog's person arrived, the park was empty. Because I was able to describe a place through this pooch's eyes, ears and nose, the dog's owner and I believed the information was correct. I used this example to show that not all lost animals are found by communicators but the information they receive shows their animal is alive and gives them hope of finding him.

My experience shows that when a lost animal is ready and wanting to be found he will be at a general location
~~~~~~~~~~~~

agreed upon between the animal and his person. The key is making certain they both are clear where that location is. I have been amazed with several lost dogs that showed at the specific rendezvous time and place agreed upon.

Scent or sight dogs whose noses or eyes rule their behavior can be headed home when suddenly they get side tracked with their seeking noses or eyes and once again are in foreign territory. To help prevent this type of dog and other animals from getting lost, or presumably lost, I believe all animals need to get their "ya ya's" out, as my friend calls it. Having their fill of the appropriate exercise and adventures, they are less likely to run away intentionally or unintentionally.

A few reasons why an animal is missing: stolen; runs from loud sounds; unhappy emotional or physical environment at home; a wild or territorial animal chases him; an indoor critter wants to escape to live outdoors; has been moved and tries to find her way back to her old home or person left behind; older animals naturally go to nature, usually a wooded area, to pass over.

Interestingly, sometimes an animal leaves home purposely so that his person will contact an animal communicator. The runaway uses this opportunity to tell his person what he wants him to know. These communications are often loving, compassionate and filled with wisdom.

Animals are aware of energy unseen or felt by many humans. Knowing this, I imagine a light beacon with strong loving energy surrounding an animal's home reaching into the sky to guide a lost animal home. Another form of using energy, created by thought, is projecting calm, loving, assertive thoughts out to them. Next envision those thoughts reaching out to the lost animal like a rope that pulls or draws him home. I believe one does not need to know physically where the lost animal is. Thinking of the animal brings the thought to them. Visualizing the lost animal walking to the front door or sitting on the back deck gives the animal an image to act on. I may use one or several of the techniques at one time. I have clients who use these methods regularly when their critters are outside and are needed at home.

Energy or thoughts are all around us. How we let them affect us impacts our lives. A good example is: You think about someone. The phone rings. It is the person you were just thinking of! The very person on your mind was thinking about you. When I share this example I wonder who thought of whom first, and how many times thinking of each other did it take for one of them to make the call. Or, how about this: Can you remember driving to the mall to buy a piece of clothing a size larger, when suddenly, you find yourself going in the opposite direction? Something has pulled you from your intended route. Lo and behold! You spy a gym and spa. Eureka! You knew all along you needed to lose those extra pounds rather than give into them. Who pulled? We don't always know, but if it feels good, go in that direction.

There are reams of books and videos on the power of thought for further understanding.

I have had several situations when the animal's person wants to search the woods or housing area his lost pet has described to me. They feel the need "to do something." From my experience, roaming the area is not always best. The animal will pick up her person's scent, and they both end up going in circles. When this happens, I ask the person to stay at a designated location and let the animal come to him, or vice versa. For guidance on which is best, I will ask the animal or listen to my intuition—or which way *feels* the best.

Lost dogs can be miles away, while cats, especially house cats, are usually close by, hiding under a deck, in a drain pipe or a pile of wood. I find when the animal is close by and wants to come home, it is because he feels threatened. The neighbor's dog, busy traffic, or an outside territorial cat, creates enough fear to cause him to stay hidden from the world. At times like these the threatened animal gives me directions and landmarks for his person to find his hideout.

One young cat told her person to listen to her meow, especially when unexpected. The college student heard her missing cat meow as she was hurrying off to classes early the next day. Kitty was a door away under a stoop. Kitty had described this place to me, but there were many places like this near her home. One would need good eyes and a flash light pointed in the exact spot she was hiding in to see her, especially at night, which was when I got the call for help.

I have had communications with lost birds. Some found their surroundings to be frightening at first, yet learned to enjoy the freedom. Some stayed close to home for a while, but eventually flew further away or did not survive due to weather or predators. My experience working with people and their renegade birds is that most people do not know the appropriate approach to entice their bird home.

I contacted Shirley Morgan, a member of the Association of Avian Veterinarians, who has attended many avian positive reinforcement conferences. Shirley has experience with a variety of birds, mostly parrots. She explained that birds react to sound and motion. Taking time to teach your bird a flock call and a recall could save your bird, if it is taught correctly. The flock call is an individual sound recognized by each species. I had to laugh, Shirley cannot whistle, so she makes a clucking sound for her flock call. Her bird clucks back! Using the flock call, one can hear the direction where the lost bird is perched.

A recall is a sound designed between you and your bird that calls the bird to fly to you. In the wild, birds fly to their flock. Shirley explained that birds are extremely visually oriented. To incorporate visual cues with sound is even more effective. An example Shirley gave was to hold your arm out, tap it and say, "Fly your wings," or "fly here." The bird is trained with these visual and verbal cues to fly to the person's arm. If an escaped bird is in a tree, he would likely fly to his person. Building trust with your bird through positive reinforcement is most important for your bird to fly to you on cue.

Shirley shared more information on escaped birds. Setting the escaped bird's cage or travel cage outside will draw it to the safety of something familiar. Birds can handle cold and wind better than people think they can. It is essential to provide food and water to a bird that has been lost. Birds do not have the muscles or skills to escape from predator birds. When a domestic bird lands on the ground, it often has undeveloped flight skills and has trouble flying upward. A bird in this situation would be a sitting target for a dog, cat or hawk. Shirley believes micro chipping is essential. If you find a bird, always check if he has been micro chipped.

For more information on understanding and teaching birds, go to, www.thebirdforum.com. Numerous references are on this site as well.

I have worked with many types of lost critters: iguanas, guinea pigs, pet rats, flying squirrels, rabbits, cats, dogs, snakes, hamsters, and more.

Not all animal communicators will work with lost animals and their people. The circumstances are the most challenging, frustrating and can be depressing. When I hear clients say they are thankful for the time, energy and emotional support I have put into helping them and their critter, which has not been found—I cringe. Happy endings are the only ones in which I can honestly say, "You're welcome."

In looking for a lost animal, first and foremost, I want to know if it has passed over or not. An animal communicator speaks to the energetic side of animals, their spirits, their thoughts. This is also the part of the animals we speak to when they have passed over; therefore, knowing if the animal is in body or not can be tricky. When I first started animal communicating, I relied on tuning into the animal's energy to sense if they were in body or out. To me, when out of body, they feel lighter, softer, or fluffy, an odd word to use, yet it fits. I later learned to ask for a sign from the animal to show me if he is in his body. The first time I asked this question to a lost dog, he showed me he can make foot prints in the mud. The dog had been seen running near a creek. During another communication, a lost cat that had passed over showed me she was floating in the trees.

If one chooses to use a communicator for a lost animal, the earlier one calls, the better the results.

45

8

Piggy Beauty Advice

"There is no cosmetic for beauty like happiness."

~Lady Blessington

Coco, short for Coconut, because her hair is like the fiber on a coconut, is a pot belly pig. She lives with Jackui' Potter, who plans to make pretty pig pottery in her spare time. Coco enjoys giving Jackui' beauty tips, even when Jackui' does not ask for them! I have been engaged in several enjoyable communications in which Coco gave advice to Jackui' on make-up, wardrobe, hair, and personal affairs. Coco fits the image of the Muppet character, Miss Piggy, a name I lovingly call her.

I have twice checked in with Miss Piggy when applying makeup and have found her taste to be impeccable. One tip that I have continued using is my dark auburn "stick," as she calls it, for eyeliner as well as lipstick, a touch for my eyebrows, and a smudge on the cheeks if I need extra color. Miss Piggy was quite pleased with herself for giving me this tip. She not only gave great makeup advice, she helped simplify my life—an on-going goal of mine. I must consult her concerning my wardrobe!

Miss Piggy spends most of her day sleeping in the laundry room on a large cushy bed. Her beauty rest is important to her. I will see if Miss Piggy has time in her schedule to offer more of her wisdom. I am curious to see what she will say.

At first, Miss Piggy has her own agenda.

I just finished my evening snack and will be settling in soon. Sleep is most important to maintain one's beauty. Karen, I do not know why you cringed at the idea of putting a pierced ring on my underbelly during our last conversation. Beauty comes in many ways. You must convince Jackui' to do this for me.

"If you remember in our conversation, Jackui' was concerned this spot could become infected, since your belly is close to the ground. I have seen pictures of you with earrings, necklaces and hats. You are a beautiful pig just the way you are."

I will be fine, and I will feel good about having a new piece of jewelry.

"You are a persuasive pig. I will give her the message."

I have to smile. She is a "pot belly pig," the location of this piece of jewelry would emphasize who she is.

"Do you have other ideas to share?"

I should expound on the fact that beauty is inside; this is where it truly counts. I will interject. When a lady or man emphasizes physically appealing traits, it makes one feel fine. It draws attention to oneself, which is "the bait." Eventually, the beauty of this person is learned on a deeper level. Most do not know how to see one from the inside first. We animals know this; you beautiful people should put your attention towards doing so. There are energies one can feel and see in and around the body, which gives us this information. It can be most gorgeous, more superb than the sparkle of fine jewelry. For example, have you stood next to someone and in doing so felt good or uncomfortable? It is similar to this, yet we perceive much more. I am aware of the colors around people; some call them auras.

If you think I have fine advice on surface colors, I can give advice on creating beautiful colors for the inside of you, too. I am a great pig with many talents. Oh, people, some of you have not figured out you, too, are great. Beauty on the outside can help with creating beauty on the inside. Snort and give yourselves a treat. Wallow in the mud, it is a heavenly experience. Get down and dirty in luscious gooey mud. Close to nature is the way, giving the skin a glow, detoxifying not only the skin but the mind as well.

"I am pleased to say, Coco, I have wallowed in the mud, not only as a child, but also on an adventure with friends to view a beaver's dam. We found ourselves wading through ankle-deep mud. My inner child kicked in and started a mud-slinging, joyful adventure that turned us all into mud goddesses. Mud from head to all ten piggies. Have you ever made mud angels? Coco, I do understand! I felt wonderful for weeks."

<div align="center">~~~~~~~~~~~~••••~~~~~~~~~~~~</div>

Animals and Universal Knowledge

For animals with the gift of gab, communication is non-stop talk, talk, talk. My mouth cannot seem to keep up with the information coming to me or my fingers cannot type fast enough as I record what I am receiving. I concentrate intently on the animal's individual words until the animal has finished. I then review the information I wrote to understand the animal's message better.

Unusual and interesting communications happen when I am connected with the animal's higher self. Opening one's mind to such information is a big step, yet my ability to tap into this realm is why some call me for a communication. I have a friend who was interested in time/space reality. When she asked this, a Shiloh shepherd with whom I had worked previously, was pleased to give my friend the information she requested. I wrote the information down hurriedly as it came: *Time—space—relevance—an equation some know—of being in the place/position one chooses to focus on. The body—here for a short period, yet eternal—enjoy it—no hurry, plenty of time. Are you doing what you love? Isn't life a blast—which is actually less time than your perception of time compared to space/reality. A butterfly has a short life, yet no shorter than your own—only your perception of his life which is a totally different reality than your own. No shorter—for much experienced. Flies are the same, even more so. Reality is—there is none. The Great All Perception.*

My friend's jaw dropped, eyes glazed over. I sensed the wheels in her head turning. She finally spoke saying, "That is a lot to ponder, and, I believe the shepherd's answer."

9

Poke a Hole and Let It Go

"So come forth into the light things, let nature be your teacher."

~Williams Wordsworth

My mother and I had a long flight from Virginia to Washington State. My brother, Dan, met us at the airport and drove us into beautiful green, lush country. The tall trees and cooling rivers we passed on our way to his home refreshed my soul.

We drove down a long gravel road where trees and plants shared their shades of green and brown with red birds decorating their branches. A home appeared at the end of the road with large wooden beams supporting the porch roof. My brother is a talented carpenter. I knew immediately the beams had been crafted by his hands. His work is respectful to the natural design a wooden beam possesses. He also builds dome homes, which are respectful to nature in conserving energy and provide a safer home to live in during hurricanes, tornadoes and other weather predicaments.

Welcoming hugs were given to Dan's blond, beautiful, German wife, Namaste, and her striking, lovable, long dark haired daughter, Nayomi. Nayomi adores Dan, in fact, Nayomi hand-picked Dan to be her new father before Namaste and Dan knew they would be a couple. When Namaste was single, she hired Dan to work on her home. At the end of each day Dan would climb into his truck and head home. But one day was different from the others. When Dan climbed into his truck, Nayomi ran to him, climbed up on the running board, looked directly at Dan through the truck's open window and said, "You're supposed to be my father." Oh, out of the mouths of babes—they know more than adults at times. That's because they are tuned in, tapped on to more than meets the eye.

We stretched our legs walking around their property, enjoying soothing gardens and water ponds decorated with bird houses made from pieces of nature Namaste had gathered. Angel figurines sitting on rocks and natural moss added to a peaceful yard. I felt as if I were in fairy land.

At the back left side of their yard stood a full scale replica of a counsel, teepee. The authenticity inside and out was impressive. I felt the urge to participate in a pow wow. To the back right was a large trampoline slightly bent across the middle. The explanation on how Dan and family presume it was bent is most extraordinary.

On Nayomi's birthday, January the fourth, several little girls had been squealing and laughing from bouncing on the trampoline and playing in the yard. Around 4:00 they decided to play in the tipi. The tipi was nestled into a wooded area with trees on three sides and the sun was now low in the sky. As they moved closer to the door of the tipi, hysteria erupted as the girls glimpsed a large shadowy figure inside. They all ran clamoring into the house. Which was wider, their mouths or eyes, is hard to say. Namaste's explanation, was there were things inside the tipi that could possibly look like a person, and to overactive imaginations; she dismissed the idea of an apparition.

The girls gave up on their story and retreated to Nayomi's bedroom to play. The girls played quietly until Namaste heard an outburst of screams, followed by clattering feet running hysterically to her in the kitchen. With fear in their voices, the girls explained that they had seen the same tall being with big, red-glowing eyes looking at them directly outside of Nayomi's bedroom window. Nayomi's window is at least eight feet high at the bottom ledge with no trees or structure to climb on.

Namaste's mother was in town getting pizza for the party while this was going on. Once the pizza arrived, the girls began to eat, and grandmother retreated to the back porch. In Namaste's words: "All of a sudden my mother yells, 'Namaste, come out here, and bring the gun!' Now my mother has never ever asked for a gun in her life, and I thought she was joking, but her voice sounded serious. When I ran out she said she heard someone or something run right by the side of the house, around the little garden into the woods and behind the tipi. Mom said, 'It—was not—a person, the footsteps were so heavy, it must have been something huge—but it definitely ran on two feet.' She got a whiff of a really unpleasant smell, a smell that their shepherd Akira sometimes comes back with after roaming in the area." They do not know where Akira gets this smell or what it is.

The next morning they found Nayomi's trampoline turned upright, wrapped around a tree. No wind or storm of any kind that night, or the next morning could have done such damage.

Namaste, Nayomi or Grandmother had never heard of Big Foot. At that time Dan and Namaste were not a couple, but once the ladies shared the incident with Dan they researched Big Foot sightings in the area and found that in the last ten years there were three sightings within a ten-mile radius of their property. They also discovered that many do not report sightings. In research, they discovered glowing eyes and a repugnant odor are associated with Big Foot. Neighbors say that twice a year, similar to migrating birds, Big Foot travels through this area. Nayomi's birthday was in this time frame.

My peaceful mood of fairies and pow wows turned curious, but not fearful, in any way. A bit discouraged, I knew in my heart a Big Foot adventure was not going to take place—at least not during this trip.

Once inside their welcoming home, I was introduced to the family bird, Butchie. I asked about this little yellow chatty bird's unusual name. Namaste explained to me that Germans lovingly give the name Butchie to birds like Americans give the name Polly. Remember the saying: Polly want a cracker?

Butchie and I immediately took a liking to each other. When released from his cage, he flew straight to my shoulder. Our first conversation pertained to little birds needing love similar to people needing love. A few days later I was uncannily drawn to Butchie's bird cage. I walked over to his cage; my eyes were drawn to the cage floor. A brilliant yellow tail feather next to a wing feather lay on the floor. This little yellow Cockatiel endeared himself by gifting me a bright yellow tail and wing feather. His family informed me that this was his first molted tail feather. Namaste felt in her heart that the feathers were a gift from Butchie. I whole-heartedly accepted his gift.

I asked Butchie why he had given me his feathers. He responded:

The wing feather is to keep you flying on your journey. It is yellow, like sunshine, to keep your spirit high and so you may actually see more than you perceive that you can. The tail feather guides. We flighted ones will help guide you in directions to serve nature, which includes you and all others. Don't give up on us; a larger purpose is at hand. While on your journey, see, think, and feel the feathers; use them as a focal point to distract you from all the jibber-jabber in your world.

"Slow down Butchie, I'm not sure I am ready for what you say!"

Nah, there could be a lot more. Enjoy the ride, until the next stop. Peace!

Approximately a week after returning home, I kept hearing, "Butchie, Butchie, Butchie Bird" over and over in my head. I finally realized what this little bird was trying to do. Butchie wanted his information put into poetry, like a conversation between the two of us.

> *Butchie, Butchie, Butchie Bird*
> *Flying high upon the words.*
> *Brings the beast to its knees.*
>
> Hey, little bird,
> Who speaks without a phone,
> If your will pleases, call!
>
> *The strength within,*
> *With feathers fly,*
> *To a place within your eye.*
>
> Butchie, Butchie, Butchie bird,
> Why be you in this place of awe?
> Singing songs, I hear your caw.
>
> *Butchie, Butchie, Butchie bird*
> *Feeds the world of golden hue,*
> *Spreading sunshine into our blue.*
>
> Butchie, Butchie, Butchie bird,
> Why do you keep pecking on my shoe?
> You irritate me, indeed you do!
>
> Butchie, Butchie, Butchie bird,
> This I say, it is a must;
> The holes you peck, a destructive touch.

Butchie, Butchie, Butchie says,
A purpose is in place,
Poke a hole to touch the soul.

Butchie, Butchie, Butchie bird,
Help me understand this deed
To release what we no longer need?

Butchie, Butchie, Butchie says,
When there is tension, release please.
Build it up, it might explode!

Butchie, Butchie, Butchie bird,
Don't you believe a beak in need
Could be the cause of this deed?

Butchie, Butchie, Butchie says,
This little beak, you see,
Could be my tension, this is key.

Butchie, Butchie, Butchie bird,
What you say I do believe.
Find your tension and relieve.

Butchie, Butchie, Butchie says,
YES, poke a hole
And let it go.

Butchie, Butchie, Butchie says,
Seeing the beast is overdue.
I'll fly to you on golden hue.

I shared Butchie's poem with my friend Jane who is knowledgeable about birds' health and behavior. She explained that when birds peck on furniture, clothes, or other things excessively, it usually means they are in need of perhaps a toy for entertainment or a different diet. They are trying to get something either for their personality or for health needs. If the problem is not remedied, their frustration or health need gets worse and so does the pecking. The pecking can become so extreme they pluck out their own feathers till they are almost bald. Their personalities seem like little "beasts," similar to when people experiencing difficulties express their frustrations in dramatic ways.

How do we bring our "beast," or destructive behaviors and fears to their knees? When Butchie said, "Poke a hole to touch the soul," he was referring to my shoe sole. A nice play on words! We walk through life on the *soles* of our feet. At times we create unhappy experiences in our walk of life which creates what Butchie calls "tension." This tension can be "destructive" to our lives and "irritating" to deal with when we try to work through it. Butchie says, "Poke a hole and let it go." When we let our tensions go, we can begin to feel lighter, both physically and emotionally. Our lives move much easier when we smile more for ourselves and others. When we shine brighter, or *"on golden hue,"* we find a more satisfying way of living.

Sometimes an animal comes into your life and offers help as Butchie did. With this understanding, he "flies" to you "on golden hue." Call him in your thoughts, and he will "caw" back.

After Butchie's communication, a variety of birds made themselves known to me. At first I would take notice of a specific breed over and over again. At times I would communicate with them for information pertaining to my life. Because I am aligned with Tom Brown's book, *Animal Speaks,* I also looked up what the bird symbolically represents. A sentence or paragraph would seem to pop off the page with information usually pertaining to another step into what I was becoming. For instance, the keynote for the sparrow is: Awakening and triumph of common nobility. Two passages that spoke to me: *It will awaken within you a new sense of dignity and self-worth, helping you to triumph in spite of outer circumstances.* The second: *There is a dark spot on each side of its throat and a heavy spot in the middle of the breast. This reflects a drawing down of energy to awaken the heart and the throat centers.*

Amazing, as I type this, a sparrow is tapping at my window, three feet away.

There were times I did not want to be responsible, accept help, or receive any kind of message from the bird kingdom. I learned if I turned my attention away or ignored a persistent bird I would find him lifeless at my doorstep. A shock to see. I found three birds—hummingbird, cardinal, and sparrow at my door. I have feathers from each one to remind me not to ignore their gifts. I learned to embrace what flew into my life. We humans tend to run from ourselves, not wanting to acknowledge our greatness, our strengths, our talents. I was one.

I realize the birds deliver messages from the Divine side. The side I need to recognize in me.

I love it—sparrow is now singing!

~~~~~~~~~~~~~••~~~~~~~~~~~~

Different Ways to Communicate

Some animal communicators prefer to be with the animal physically during the communication. Others prefer a picture of the animal, and some need only a phone, a person to talk to, and the name and description of an animal to focus on. Some may ask for questions concerning the animal, then put themselves in a meditative state, receive the answers, and then call or email the person back to give the answers. When I communicate on the phone, the location of the animal and person does not matter; they can be in different countries, or in the same room.

I have laughed to myself more than once when asked if the phone should be held to the animal's ear! I have communicated with a person calling from Korea while her horse was in Maryland.
~~~~~~~~~~~~~

10

True Power

"Let a man decide upon his favorite animal and make a study of it. Let him learn to understand its sounds and motions. The animals want to communicate with man. But Wakean-Tanka does not intend that they should do so directly. Man must do the greater part in securing an understanding."

~Brave Buffalo, Standing Rock Reservation

While I was enjoying my ride on a tram in a wildlife park in Washington State, a large bull elk made himself known to me. The tram had stopped for us visitors to watch a magnificent herd of about twenty elk. The elk were grazing in a natural setting of rolling hills, green pasture and wooded areas, the way nature intended. They seemed to be content, at peace.

The largest bull elk walked towards the tram but stopped about ten feet away and stared directly at me. He then, with intent, walked to where I sat. The elk's proud head, crowned with extremely large antlers, was getting too close for our driver's comfort so he promptly moved the tram forward. I knew elk's actions could not be ignored; I would communicate with him at a later date.

At home with my trusty laptop, I telepathically connected to elk and prepared to type his words.

He quickly bellowed, *WHAT DO YOU WANT?*

"I am collecting information from animals, giving them an opportunity to be heard. Would you like to add your thoughts?"

Can I say anything?

"Yes, anything."

You people are almost helpless. You have no idea what it means to be one with nature—Nature Park, bah! You don't get down and close; you act as if you are watching a TV screen. Feel our treatment of one another, our order in which we revere life. We know when to give life and when to let go. Let go, let go, you fools. Go into the body of an elk, feel the vibrations of earth under our feet. Know the presence of power, true power. It is not who has more stock or money in the bank.

This is useless. You people will drive by in your little tram and gawk at the scenes.

"You have strong feelings, and I appreciate your concerns. Do you have more to say?"

Yes . . . just . . . good luck with your book. I hope it gets through to some of those gawking people!

"I will do my best so others may hear your message."

Okay, okay, get on with it.

~~~~~~~~~~~~•••~~~~~~~~~~~~

X-Ray Vision

My library of anatomy charts comes in handy when I do a body scan. I can actually see inside the animal's body, similar to an x-ray. I see in my mind's eye what the liver, a broken bone, or a torn ligament looks like by focusing my thoughts on that particular area. My job is to describe the problem and leave the rest to the experts.

A show horse had consistently come up lame. The veterinarian and farrier had worked on the condition several times without success. In all three of our communications in regards to the same subject, the horse always gave the same answer: *a small chip of bone is in my fetlock joint*. I could see this little irritating splinter when I scanned his joint. Eventually, after great frustration between people and the horse, he was trailered to a specialist. The specialist found the irritating chip during an operation and corrected the problem. Human and horse were off to shows once again.

Scanning the body like an ex-ray machine may seem a bit far-fetched to some, but many can learn to do it. Pretend you are seeing the inside of the body, make believe, fake it until you eventually "see it." Our minds are wonderful; they can travel through time and space…anywhere we want. Try scanning a person who can validate what you receive or an animal when a person or vet can validate your information. You might surprise yourself.
~~~~~~~~~~~~

11

Tots and Toys

"We can judge the heart of a man by his treatment of animals".

~Immanuel Kant

My brother Dan and his family planned a trip for my mother and me to tour a nature park while visiting them in Washington State. The weather in the Seattle area is usually rainy or damp, but this day was clear and crisp. Once inside the park, I was drawn to a small group of children, seven to twelve years old, watching two raccoons in a small enclosure. One raccoon was next to a large glass panel separating him by inches from the children. I walked closer and noticed the raccoons were more intensely watching the children than the children were watching the raccoons. There was definitely a communication to be had here!

The raccoon closest to the glass pane anxiously wanted to be heard:

Hi there, I want you to know I'm so tired of being the exhibit of others and people being on exhibit for us. Hum, I guess it could be, we are equal in this "view."

They do supply us with adequate food, yet I know others want to choose foods "they" want to eat. This whole zoo type atmosphere seems okay if our living area is healthy and it helps people to respect us and learn. I really doubt if it's making an impact the way I would like. I see only money in the eyes of those that created this place.

I do get bored. Same old, same old. New adventures would enhance our health.

I would like to think these people are looking at our beauty and learning. I sometimes believe the young ones look at us as if we are some type of animation. Therefore, they view nature the same way and do not get the balance or health provided for them. They are disconnected, so to speak. Poor, poor, things. Perhaps this little plot of cage is better!

No, we are both in a predicament. Oh dear, what to do!

After a short silence I thought raccoon had finished his message. He had just begun!

My message about the children was quite powerful. Some don't see or experience nature the way it was intended. The young ones have false or fake activities going on in their minds and hearts. Exercising the mind creates growth in some cases; it deadens or puts false information in other circumstances. As I said earlier, money is the main priority. How much is made on those gadgets they play with? Too much time is spent with strange-looking electronic games.

Nature creates an overall calmness or balance that enhances the ability to live life, rewarding man and animal. Children, I notice most of all, instinctively want this. Life, the way it is today, pushes or gently moves them into this electronic way of life. Many parents know no better. Perhaps they should be with nature more themselves. Perhaps that is why they came to see me!

We must seek balance in all things. In my younger years I was immersed with nature. Now I am using computers and electronic gadgets writing about nature and balance.

Raccoon was not done. I think I interrupted him.

Children should be given the right to live life, moving in directions "they" need to go, furthering their personal growth. I hope they will find their path, not what others want to make them. Some animals feel they are treated this way.

"Mr. Raccoon, thank you for giving us this information. Is there more?"

It has been a pleasure speaking with you. Expressive are we raccoons. I could chatter on and on. Please keep in touch so we may share lots more. Having a voice with people has been most enjoyable. Perhaps you'll come see me again.

"Would love to."

The other raccoon, smaller in size was silent; her heart was heavy, as if depressed. She expressed, *I like it when it rains,* then became silent once again.

I asked the larger raccoon if his friend was feeling well.

Perhaps we will have babies so she will have something to look forward to! Now that would be another subject!

~~~~~~~~~~~~~•••~~~~~~~~~~~~

Being Responsible

I learned a valuable lesson when I was not being responsible with my information received; I sent the wrong cat to a home whose beloved cat had been missing for two weeks. The missing cat was yellow with white feet. I kept seeing a cat like the lost one, yet he had white up to his elbows, not just his feet. I let it pass because this cat described the outside surroundings of the home in which the
~~~~~~~~~~~~~

lost cat lived. The cat said he was in the red barn to the right of their house in the neighbor's back yard. We finished the communication and I waited.

The cat's family called back shortly. A cat, yellow with white up to its elbows, had walked up their sidewalk towards their front door. This cat was doing as told, yet it was the wrong cat. After petting the cat, they followed him to a red barn in their neighbor's yard. I opened the communication again. I thanked the cat for being so obliging in our communication, told him he should stay with his family, and then connected with the family's cat that had white only on his paws. Their cat was farther away, and he came home the next morning. This time I communicated with the correct cat. The writing was on the wall—or should I say—his legs?

12

Spay and Neuter Who

"The cat has complete emotional honesty—an attribute not often found in humans."

~Ernest Hemingway

Rosie and Josie are two remarkable calico cats I met in Washington State. They live in a pristine forest with ferns as tall as I am and trees so big it would take several people holding hands to wrap their arms around their giant trunks. Rosie and Josie cherish the great outside and roam where they wish. They respect themselves, their person Dan and the land they live on. Their job is being a companion to Dan and keeping rodents out of his home while gone. I prefer to call his abode, Dan's personal sanctuary. His home is unique, nestled in with nature, made and designed by Dan to honor the environment. Elk can roam in the backyard and cougar prowl at night. To understand how special this spot on the planet is, one would have to experience it.

As I soaked in the heavenly presence of Rosie and Josie's existence, Josie came forward and wondered what I was doing. I explained, and asked if she would like to be included in my communications. Josie asked why she would want to. I explained she could express herself to her person; Josie felt she already had an understanding. I suggested she bring up a topic of concern or a belief.

Liking my last suggestion, Josie quickly and with great intent pounced on the opportunity:

What's the big fuss about being spayed or neutered? Perhaps if people practiced it like they enforce it upon us animals, we could control the population with their species, too. Think about it! You humans could participate in life, fulfilling your multitude of needs, rather than a sheer basic existence.

In thought, Josie showed me pictures of New York City, Bangkok, Mexico City, and other areas heavily populated with unhealthy conditions. She proceeded to show me areas where people are concerned about there being too many cats. Comparing the two, the cat colonies didn't seem to be as large a problem as the number of people and how they were living.

Josie spoke again. *Did you ever think we cats would have concerns with crowded people areas? How can people bring kids into this world when their own lives are out of balance? Chaos + Chaos = Chaos. OUT OF BALANCE!*

When people have difficulties dealing with their own lives in this busy, crowded world, how can they guide a child? Are people needing to be spayed and neutered to help this situation? I'm a firm believer in taking time to know

yourself, be happy within, comfortable in your walk of life. Then show the young ones a balanced way of life. Being a mess can create a bigger mess.

I thanked Josie for giving us an interesting view from her feline perspective.

Karen, would you please thank Dan for taking care of Rosie and me in his special way?

"Consider it done."

~~~~~~~~~~~~•••~~~~~~~~~~~~

Not Enough Info

When dealing with animals that give little information, or when I don't comprehend what they are trying to tell me, I must think creatively. At times animals do not feel comfortable sharing their thoughts with me. This behavior can be a reflection of their person. When this happens, I share something about myself and explain what I can do to help them so they may learn to trust and have confidence in me. Some animals have a difficult time expressing themselves, similar to how some people have difficulty communicating. By asking questions in different ways, I give them openings to express themselves differently, and/or for me to receive the communication in new and helpful ways to understand them.

Take the story of Tom, a large tabby cat, who started urinating on his people's bed. This cat expressed himself very clearly—*I am pissed off at my people* and then boldly demonstrated his dissatisfaction in the household.

A similar yet different story involved a little timid cat, Sofia, who urinated on the side of the bed where the man of the house slept. She could only convey she was upset and frustrated, and could not explain why. It was then I asked a variety of questions to help her express herself. Have your
~~~~~~~~~~~~

people hurt you? She answered in a hesitant voice, *No.* Does this have anything to do with your food? *No.* My instincts told me it had something to do with her people. I asked if she was worried about someone she loved. *Yes.* She was not sure she should tell me because it was something her people were hiding from others. She eventually showed me in my mind's eye, similar to a little movie, several incidents of abuse happening between the man and woman with whom she lived. Her message was a wake-up call to the woman. Soon afterword the couple separated. I have often found that people may not take that big step to well-being for themselves, yet when it affects their animal, they find the courage to do so.

13

Zip It

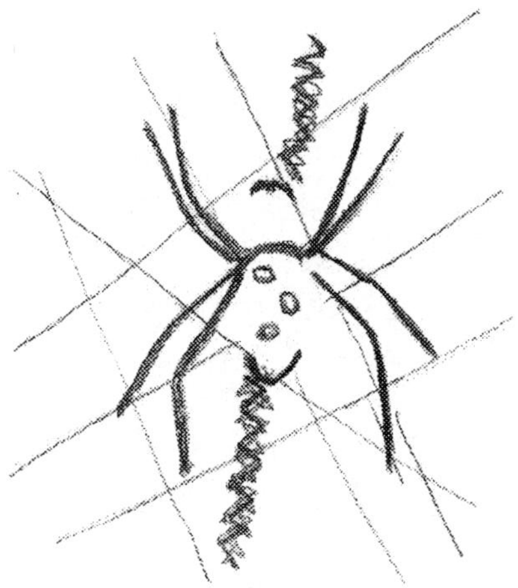

"It is man's sympathy with all creatures that first makes him truly a man. Until he extends his circle of compassion to all living things, man will not himself find peace."

~Albert Einstein

Face to face with a large black and yellow hairy spider, I was a bit daunted, especially since it took me by surprise. This lady was weaving an unusual vertical zigzag stitching in the middle of her web. I had been helping my friend Ginny clean her flower garden when Miss Spider made herself known. Ginny explained to me that because this spider weaves a prominent zigzag through its web, it is called a Zipper Spider.

Before heading home, I used the bathroom, or the "lou," as my British friend calls it. Wouldn't you know, the side zipper on my pants would not zip up. Annoyed, I pulled and tugged trying to get the blasted thing up. As I yanked on my zipper I gasped, *what is going on with zippers*? Ginny shared her belief that things come in threes if there is something to be learned.

To no surprise, Ginny and I discovered another Zipper Spider as we walked to my car. What is the message, what is to be learned? My eyebrows wrinkled and my head cocked awaiting the answer. At that moment I remembered several times when giving an animal communication and there was a need for compromise, my hands seemed to have a mind of their own. Both hands would go up in front of me, fingers up, palm to palm with the tip of my pinky fingers touching. This spot touching represents the connection between two individuals, needing teamwork. The fingers folded into each other one at a time representing giving and taking, working differences out. The fingers zipped together create unity.

I now call this action the zipper effect; at times I simply say, "zip it." I have to be careful not to say "zip it," to those who do not understand this is a good expression, not a smart-alecky one.

In my case, one pinky finger represents helping others with what they need and the other was taking time for my book and other projects working as an animal communicator and as an intuitive. I needed to find a balance of time and energy between the two. I was allowing myself to be pulled in directions with people and activities to the point that I was not respecting myself, my book, or my purpose in life being an animal communicator.

Spider's information came in a different way than other communications in this book. Yet—it works. Spider, which is part of nature, part of the Big Aha, God, Universal

Knowledge, whatever you want to call this force, supports us. Zipper Spider and I rendezvoused at a time I had become frustrated and needed help. The "zipper effect" gave me ideas on how to work out my conflict. I let go of the frustration, which was using up my energy, and took action solving the problem, which gave me energy. A little spider reminded me to spin my own web.

After my encounter with Spider, I was drawn to my *Animal-Speak* book written by Ted Andrews, which shares what creatures symbolize. I immediately went to the section on spiders. There were several pages but the last sentence is what spoke to me. *Spider can teach how to use the written language with power and creativity, so that your words weave a web around those who would read them.*

A few weeks after my close encounter with Spider, my husband's work took us to Virginia Beach. Not a surprise. When one claims what she wants and then, lets go and lets God, life changes. While John was on his appointments, my fingers flew over the key board tapping away with vigor on this book and other projects. I was thankful I was now true to myself, true to what my "gut" was trying to tell me. My creativity flowed. Spider also represents creativity.

I now had balance in my life. I had "zipped it."

If the "zip it" philosophy is used with individuals, businesses, communities, counties, state, and national government—what kind of world we would live in!

Thank you, Zipper Spider.

~~~~~~~~~~~~~~••~~~~~~~~~~~~~

Helping with Changes

Giving detailed information helps both critters and people make decisions or move through changes. When
~~~~~~~~~~~~~~

moving, remodeling, going on vacation, or doing anything that makes changes in the lives of your animals, it is important that you explain to them what is taking place. Sending your thoughts to them (through pictures, words, or feelings) and giving them time frames can help them better understand. This will make the situation easier for both you and your critter.

I received a call from a family living in Maryland who planned to move to Africa. The family wanted to give their cat and dog the choice of staying in Maryland or going with them to Africa. I explained to the critters what was soon going to happen. Their home furnishings would be packed, next they would stay in a hotel room, and then they would take a long plane flight to Africa. I gave them time frames when each stage of moving would take place. With the help of their people, I then gave them a description of their new home and how living in Africa would be different from living in Maryland. This information helped the confused cat and dog understand the situation in order to make their decision. Knowing they would be safe with their family during the trip and understanding they would live in a large beautiful home to run and play in with their devoted people were the major factors in their decision to move to Africa.

I received an email a few weeks after the family arrived in Africa. Their animals had handled the move well, and their dog loved running up and down the long stairways in their large home—something he was looking forward to from our conversation.

Usually critters have lots of questions or requests surrounding change. Where will they sleep? Will they eat the same foods? Will their people be with them when traveling? Many want belongings of importance to be with them—a toy, blanket, or a special collar they like. I have found during times when people and critters are separated, a piece of clothing or a pillowcase with the scent of their person is comforting. In this case, catnip was a request from kitty while traveling on the plane!

During times when we have to be away from our loved critters, we can be with them in spirit or in thought. While traveling, people can send pictures in their minds to their animals, holding and loving them as if they were with them. Their animals definitely receive comfort from these messages. The better state of mind the family or person is in, the better for the critter. If the family is worried and upset, the animal picks up on the mood and reflects it. This is no different from how a person's bad mood or a happy mood affects the emotions of others around them. Animals stressed due to separation anxieties will weather the situation much better if the owners use positive emotions and thought pictures. Thoughts are powerful; use them wisely.

14

Needing Mother's T.L.C

"When God created the horse he said to the magnificent creature: I have made thee as no other. All treasures of the earth lie between thy eyes. Thou shalt carry my friends upon they back. Thy saddle shall be the seat of prayers to me. And thou fly without wings, and conquer without any sword. Oh, horse."

~The Qu'ran (Koran)

Cribbing is when a horse grabs an object with his teeth, neck arched, gulping air. This behavior can wear down the teeth and swallowing air can lead to digestion and colic problems. Cribbing, chronic lameness problems, and nervous behavior in stalls can be troublesome problems for some horses. During my communication with a show horse named

Howdy, the reasons why he has these problems were revealed.

In my conversation with Howdy, he continually showed me his upper leg area while we were addressing a problem of his being lame in his right front leg. This was not the first time he had come up lame. Every time he got better, eventually the same problem or a new one appeared. The trainer, farrier, and vet all claimed the problem was in his hoof. Each time Howdy persisted by showing me his extensor muscles, the ones between the elbow and the knee. However, no one could find anything wrong with this area.

Frustrated, I decided to look in another direction. I asked Howdy what the core issue was behind this problem. He immediately sent a picture of a colt nursing his mother, stretching his neck, and coordinating the different muscles of his body. He further showed me the position of his legs while he nursed, and how muscles throughout his body were utilized differently as he grew. As he grew taller, his legs would bend and his body would shift more and more in order to reach his mother's milk. He expressed the importance of experiencing security and love between a mother and her baby in order for the baby to become a well-balanced adult horse. He was separated from his mother at three and a half months, and the lack of that extra mental and emotional support as Howdy grew affected him in later years.

Before Howdy could continue, his owner Fran Ichijo, whom I was giving the communication to, blurted "Cribbing!" Howdy was also a cribber. The bigger picture was coming together. Howdy showed us that weaning him too early had created an array of problems, including his cribbing and chronic lameness problems in his front legs and hooves. At that moment, in my mind, a picture flashed of Howdy nervously weaving back and forth in his stall, a habit resulting from the anxiety of being separated from his mother too early. As he grew older, these anxieties from his earlier years reappeared each time he was separated from horses, people, or other connections which gave him security. Man's early intervention between mother and foal was not in tune with nature.

Fran gave instances of other horses that would start cribbing when stalled next to a cribber. An example of a happy horse is Fran's two-year-old, Tara. Even with cribbers on both sides, Tara has never cribbed; she exhibits a pleasant personality, and accepts the bridle and saddle nicely. Tara was born on Fran's farm and was weaned after six months, not four like many foals. She still had contact with her mother after she was weaned.

According to Howdy's information, weaning at a later stage results in a horse that is physically and mentally better prepared for its journey in life, which benefits both horse and person. Allowing a foal to stay longer with its mother is the loving thing to do. Mothers, fathers, and children with a healthy relationship are happier and adjust to life's stresses with less conflict. The same holds true for horses.

Howdy's lameness was chronic at that time but was soon relieved. Now that we understood Howdy's unhappy emotional patterns, which affected him physically, we began to find ways to help him. I have found animals release emotions and behaviors more quickly than humans. Sometimes the simple act of expressing themselves will change the problem. I was hoping this would be true with our special boy. To support his need for a more balanced, happier mind I also worked with Howdy on the emotional level to help him release unwanted conditioning he had acquired in life, in exchange for a happier future. On the physical level, Fran found an excellent farrier who provided Howdy with the appropriate hoof care and horseshoes. Howdy is now a much happier horse; his spirit soars, especially over jumps.

I am not saying that later weaning will banish all problems. Horses are asked to jump higher, run faster, stop faster, and turn quicker as competitions intensify. They perform in ways that look physically impossible, and they have no personal input on what saddle or bridle they wear. They cannot choose their living conditions, their training, or their riders. These factors might unknowingly cause damage, even from people who have the highest respect for their horses. However, a sounder and happier horse is better equipped to endure life and perform in the many tasks people demand.

I have to interject that some animals are understood by their trainers, groomers, and those that shape their lives. Horses and other animals have many ways to show people what they want and need outside of using an animal communicator. Their behavior is many times understood, but they also influence those around them with their thoughts that people receive, even if the people do not perceive it is the horse projecting the information.

Using common sense, we can apply the information Howdy shared with me to all animals. Animals do not like physical or emotional pain any more than we do. As their caregivers, we should respect our animal companions and care for them in a compassionate manner.

~~~~~~~~~~~~~~•••~~~~~~~~~~~~~

Animals Attracting People

I have found animals can attract the type of people they wish to be with. I have heard many stories from people who ventured out looking for a specific breed or type of critter and then were drawn to an animal outside of their thinking. Dean was focused on finding a dog at an animal rescue building, but when his eyes met with a beautiful long-haired calico cat he fell in love. Dean substituted a bark for a meow. Driving down a road seeing a sign selling pups, Carol made an unexpected u-turn. Her logic was, "I'm just curious." She fell in love with a pup and took her home. It is not unusual for something unexpected to grab our attention going down
~~~~~~~~~~~~~~

the road of life. To investigate the diversion could bring a blessing, a wish come true. Are they accidents? I think not.

Many can relate to a time when they wake to an animal sitting on the door step which turns out to be perfect for their household. Why did the stray pick your door and not the neighbors? Because *you* were inside.

15

Feeling Small

"Nature will bear the closest inspection. She invites us to lay our eye level with her smallest leaf, and take an insect view of its plain."

~Henry David Thoreau

An ant was found in the exact spot on the corner of LeAndra's bathroom counter each morning for three days in a row. Each day the ant was the same size, same color and position. LeAndra wondered why she was having this unusual ant encounter. So, she called me—in this case, an ant communicator!

Ant began to speak:

So, I am small. Do you feel this way sometimes? Sure you do, and that is okay. Look at the universe, so big and vast. When you look up at the sky, what you see is tiny compared to what you don't see. There is more than most can imagine.

Have you ever cut the tip of your finger or had a little splinter in your skin? Hurt like the dickens! The whole body knew it! So, it was important, that tiny little place.

Importance, what is that? Something you may have forgotten, until it was gone. Or that tiny little place that hurts—it becomes very important. Are you important, tiny little thing? Yes.

Many think of importance like a ladder—those at the top are most important, those at the bottom the least. Take the ladder and turn it sideways. Now what do we have?

"Thank you, Ant. May I recap what you have said?"

This is an important message, do what it takes for those to understand.

"I will do my best."

If you feel tiny and insignificant in this world, remember you are immensely important to God and to yourself, no matter who you are or what you do. Recognize your attributes, appreciate your life, everything you do, everything you are, good, bad, or ugly, are part of the grand picture of why we are on earth. Live and love life the best you know how. You—tiny little speck in the universe—are very important. It is up to *you* to be responsible to believe in yourself, no matter what.

~~~~~~~~~~~~~••~~~~~~~~~~~~~

An Animal's Purpose

Animals need a job or purpose in life. I communicate to them how much their person appreciates their watching over the house, their unconditional love and companionship, or
~~~~~~~~~~~~~

for irritating you when they know you have been sitting too long at the computer! Giving animals a job or a specific purpose can help them feel better and help change bad habits.

A black lab fostered from a rescue organization in Maryland barked ferociously while running up and down a chain link fence on one side in his back yard. The lab then showed me the opposite side of the fenced yard. It was made of wood—he never barked on that side. His foster people validated this and his growling at the family members who walked by him while he rested in a secluded corner. The lab's family had hope that he could be a happy, content dog. I answered their call for help.

This black lab showed me in pictures and feelings what his life was like before he was taken to the animal shelter. His past job had been to alert the household at all times when there was any kind of activity near the house. He showed me in mental pictures a small home surrounded by a chain link fence. Inside the largest room of this house were long tables with people sitting at them, cutting something grassy and green, dividing it, and putting it into bags. Everyone living in the house and those coming and going from it were tense and overly mindful of their surroundings. I came to the conclusion this was drug related.

The responsibility given to this dog was extreme. I then explained to this heavy-hearted, tense lab what life could be like for him now and what had happened in the past no longer had to control him. I sent him examples with everything I could conjure up to show him his job was to relax, enjoy life, be loved, and give love. I sent feelings, words and pictures of being petted, doted over, playing, and having fun with different family members in order to give him the total experience. I asked this family to hold only these thoughts I had sent their dog. If he even starts to act like the old dog, give him a good but gentle reminder he has a new job. Send feelings of being safe, relaxed and enjoying life.

Good news came soon after. The family informed me the next day they had a transformed dog. An animal can change his behavior quickly. In this case, an entire family was on board holding good thoughts which greatly helped. He had started to bark at the chain link fence only one time, after our communication, so the husband did as advised—he reminded the lab of his new life and that he was safe. The dog immediately stopped in his tracks. The growling also stopped. Now he enjoys lying belly up on the living room floor. Thank goodness this story had a happy ending. Many times when dogs behave aggressively, without intervention, the dogs are euthanized.

16

Be in Peace

"The poor dog, in life, the firmest friend, the first to welcome, foremost to defend."

~Lord Byron

I settled into a large, soft comfortable chair, my legs curled up under me as I began to relax and wonder when my next communication would be, and with what kind of animal. Unexpectedly, I became aware of someone alerting my mental attention. I sat upright, my mind expanding, and trying to grasp something recognizable. Usually, one of my senses can recognize who the animal is. On this day, I seemed to be in a fog. I asked, "Who is this?" I barely saw an image of a small, long-haired white dog.

I welcomed White Dog and asked why he was calling me. He immediately communicated on a topic he wanted to share.

Some people just don't enjoy life the way they could. Busy, busy, busy in life, not knowing what's going on. What's the real stuff that makes life worthwhile? Behold the raindrop, a rose petal, or a stone in a field. One will "see and be" so much more!

Be in peace every moment and your life will serve you true.

"I'm pleased you made yourself known."

With the blink of my eye, White Dog was gone!

I later realized this was the same White Dog that had mysteriously showed up, and left as quickly, during a previous difficult time. A few years earlier, when I became known as an animal communicator, I had an unexpected phone call. A reporter wanted to interview me regarding an engagement where I would be a guest speaker. Not yet accustomed to dealing with the media, I was nervous and did not express myself the way a seasoned communicator would have. The reporter made condescending remarks about my beliefs and the way I handled myself. I felt vulnerable and began to believe the reporter was right, that I was not capable of what it takes to be a communicator in the public eye. Since I take my communications seriously, I can't afford to be self-doubting when dealing with lost, sick, or dying animals. At this point, however, I felt weak and insecure and wasn't sure if I had the courage to speak to a group of people. I needed to be on my toes for this one, yet I was deflated. Tears came to my eyes.

Suddenly a little white dog appeared in my mind and soothed my soul. He said to me, *Do not fear what that lady said—she doesn't know what she is talking about! Bringing about change is not always gentle.* He reminded me that some people strike out at others when they don't understand or can't accept a new way of being. It can be frightening. In my case, animal communication was not within her comfort zone. White Dog then said, *It would be best to forgive and get on with what is at hand.* He then quickly disappeared, leaving me feeling safe. I was thankful for this little white dog; his wisdom gave me the courage to believe in who I am, and to speak effectively about animal communication.

~~~~~~~~~~~~••~~~~~~~~~~~

Ur-in-it

Animals not only have their own interests at heart but their person's interest as well. While I was giving communications at an engagement, I helped a slender little dog give his large, muscular person information to hopefully change his life for the better.

Chip, a miniature pinscher, wore a black leather, spiked collar. He stood proud and still like a beautiful sculpture where he was placed on a table between his person, Dave, and me. A miniature Goliath, I first thought. They had been waiting two hours for their communication. All of my appointments at this appearance were booked yet he was willing to wait and see if Chip and he could be seen. I had stayed over the determined time to give communications and was now in my seventh hour. I was running on empty. After days like these, I need two days to recuperate. People kept coming on this dreary, rainy day; some had driven from over an hour away with critter in tow. I could not turn them away. I have been known to continue giving communications when doors are closing or tents are being taken down around me.

I thought I was finished for the day until I saw Dave. He was sitting in a chair against the far wall with Chip. I learned he had let others go ahead of him. I was asked, "Could I see one more?" When I saw Chip and Dave, my energy spiked. I
~~~~~~~~~~~~

was tuned in, tapped on, ready to do whatever it took for this communication.

Dave informed me that Chip often messed on the kitchen floor while he was at work. Even though Chip was let outside two or three times a day, Chip was not behaving. Looking into Chip's big brown eyes, I learned Dave spent little time at home. Dave explained he had a full-time day job and worked another job a few hours at night. Urinating on the floor was Chip's way of saying, "I am not happy."

I had communicated with another dog earlier that month that had urinated on his person's leg, and when asked why, he said, *Ur-in-it!* An outburst of laughter followed his answer. We immediately realized what he was conveying. He made a play on the word urine to show that the dog's life and person's life evolved around each other. You're in "it," or you're in my life. Look at your life and let us see why our lives are not as good as they could be. This dog was a big Doberman—big puddle, with a big message. Through the communication he gave guidance to his person, and insights to his needs as well, on how to create a happier life together. And now I was about to hear Chip's view.

Dave told me he lives by himself and that he got Chip for companionship, yet Dave was rarely home during the week to keep his pup happy. This smart little dog solved the problem; Chip suggested that his person bring him to his first job of the day. This was doable. Man's best friend could now be by his side, and fulfill his second job—babe catcher! Oh, and pooch asked that when he was dressed in his Harley Davidson jacket: *Please turn up the collar—much more attractive—the babes like it!* Chip knew his person wanted a serious female companion in his life. Companionship seemed to be the dominant topic!

This little mini pin's information was surprising to his owner, but a greater surprise came when Chip told me that Dave was a bouncer by night. This bit of news made Dave sit back in his chair with his eyes and mouth open. He was now concerned about what else his little friend might reveal.

Chip discreetly explained how his person needed a reality check on how he was running his life. Two jobs not only left a little dog lonely, they left his person lonely as well. Dave now looks at his little critter with different eyes. At the end of our communication, Dave thought about this unexpected knowledge from his little wise guy. He realized he needed to make changes in his life in order to pursue what was important to him. In this case, looking for puppy love came in two forms; two footed and four footed. Spending more time with Chip, especially when suited up with his Harley jacket, would also attract "the babes." A win win situation.

If owners act on changes suggested by an animal, life improves. People can get stuck in a routine. In this case, a diminutive mini pin supported and encouraged a big, burly bouncer to make positive changes.

Animals use some interesting tactics to make a point, especially when their people least expect it.

17

Kitty Knows Best

"If man could be crossed with the cat, it would improve man, but it would deteriorate the cat."

~Mark Twain

Pretty Girl was a little kitty lost in a grove of trees behind her family's townhouse. Having moved two months ago from a small farm in Maryland, she was not sure of her way home. Under a bush outside her front door was the farthest she had ventured from her new home. If a car passed by, her four paws hurriedly dashed her inside to safety. On this day, the door—which was always kept open for her—had shut. Pretty Girl now had to improvise on how to survive outside, as her family improvised on how to survive inside. Several hours passed before her people noticed Pretty Girl was missing. I received a frantic telephone call, for this little gray cat was more than a pet—she was helping the family through a divorce.

Via telepathy, I located Pretty Girl among the shrubs and trees behind their townhouse, but she was determined not to move—as if her feet were stuck to the ground. She had never been in the back yard. I explained to her where the back door to their home was, and that her family was waiting there for her. I knew she was close by and understood how to find her way home. After I ended the phone conversation I began to feel restless, incomplete with the communication. I sensed her feet were still stuck to the ground. I opened myself to outside guidance. I believe my higher self, or a group of spiritual beings as in angels, guides or evolved beings assist me. It came to me to ask them what I could do in order to unglue Pretty Girl's feet from the ground and prompt her to go home. Immediately she piped in: *I want you to write down what I am about to say.*

I grabbed paper and pencil and began writing fast and furious, trying not to miss a word. She spoke in short phrases: *Buy the son a watch, let the daughter decorate her room the way she wants, encourage the son to have friends over,* and other trivial to serious advice. Later I found the information Pretty Girl gave were topics the mother had been thinking about but was uncertain as to what to do. Receiving the simpler, less serious information first, she provided credence to the more disturbing information that came later concerning divorce and children. Pretty Girl conveyed she was concerned for the children, especially a possible kidnapping by the father, now living in another country. I later learned the mother had indeed worried the children might be kidnapped by their father and kept in his country under his law.

After I'd filled two long pages of information from Pretty Girl, there was a pause. I thought she had finished and I was about to say, "Are you ready to head home?" Instead, her reply caught me off guard. *I will not go home unless you put me in the book you are writing.*

I could not believe what I heard. I double checked. I'd heard correctly. I contemplated this request for a nano-second and realized she had me in a corner. When I communicated with Pretty Girl, I had lost my drive to write for several months. My friends and family had strongly encouraged me to write again, now a cat! It was early winter and getting colder every moment now that it was dark outside. I considered Pretty Girl's safety and agreed.

Pretty Girl's commanding request worked for both of us. My phone rang five minutes after I consented to her wishes; the family had called to report that Pretty Girl was home. Mom followed through with Pretty Girl's suggestions. A year later I heard the children were safe and sound. As for me, I now had a reason to continue with my book.

Now that the little manipulator had motivated me, I asked P.G. (a nickname I gave her, as in the movie rating parental guidance) if she was ready for her début.

She told me to take a break. I don't like sitting for long periods of time, and she knew how long I had been talking on the phone with her people as well as writing two pages of information from her for her people. Perhaps I shouldn't be so perturbed with her little stunt! She was being a con-siderate kitty.

Break time was over. I reconnected with P.G.

I would like to share with you a common interest of many. Life is too short to live it in fear—fear is the main beast behind all our problems.

No, forget that life is too short not to live it in laughter, joy, pretending, using your imagination. A crazy, fun life— no problems. You are what you think, so think what you want, hold it, or be it, and it is yours. Got it? Now go have fun. Unless you think all is bad and depressing, then go be that.

"Is there more?"

No, I think that is enough for most. Some may not get it, so read this several times until you do and then check to see how you are living your life. There!

Karen, I thank you for respecting my wishes, it will benefit many. Nature works in strange ways, as you have found—no coincidences in this world. Now, go play, or live life, or be alive in life, or just be, knowing the whole world is yours and you are greatly loved.

I am now done with my "parental guidance."

"P.G., you are one tricky kitty, a special tricky kitty."

~~~~~~~~~~~~~~•••~~~~~~~~~~~~~

Information Not Shared

On a local T.V. show I once communicated with a young black cat who described what type of person she wanted to adopt her from the humane society. I heard she wanted a young girl to be her companion. As I was expressing what the cat had just told me, ever so faintly, I heard the cat say an older lady would be nice, too. I did not mention this new information, for I heard it at the same time I was talking. Immediately, the TV host began asking other questions, and at the time it appeared I was unable to wedge in this new information. As it turned out, an older lady living by herself adopted the little black kitten.

To give information on a TV show where I appeared to be wrong—I admit, my ego was damaged. My experience was not a pleasant way to learn the lesson of sharing all of the information an animal gives. As I look back, I could have worked kitty's added information into our conversation. I was nervous being on TV. My experience, without doubt, was one that impacted my performance as a communicator, on, and off of TV. Thank goodness it was not a critical mistake.
~~~~~~~~~~~~~~

18

It Is What It Is

"In almost everything that touches our everyday life on earth, God is pleased when we're pleased. He wills that we be as free as birds to soar and sing our maker's praise without anxiety."

~A. W. Tozer

"On the road again" has been my favorite saying lately. Between my husband's business and visiting family, our car has become our part-time home. Fortunately, I can give animal communications as long as I have a phone. While in Northern Virginia, I gave an emergency communication in the middle of Lowe's building supply store. Thank you, God, for cell phones.

Our travels have taken us to Virginia Beach with my husband's work. We enjoy watching the dolphins each morning and evening as they swim and play past our hotel window. They have earned their fame by saving many lives at sea; in addition, their interaction with people has proven to be therapeutic in many ways. Today, they are simply happy-go-lucky creatures to watch and enjoy.

While John, my husband, is at work, I type intently at my laptop until I realize my sore behind needs relief from sitting too long. I feel blessed the beach is available to stretch my legs. I toss my shoes off and beeline to the ocean edge. My feet sink into the sand as an ocean wave plays with me. I look to the ocean to see dolphins surfing the waves. I revere these divine creatures, yet it is the pelican that intrigues me today.

I watch the pelicans fly, twelve in a row, following a wave only inches below their body. The tips of their graceful wings tap the surface of the water as they pursue a surging wave on its course. As I observe these spectacular birds, I realize the pelican's movement is similar to the dolphins, though one is in air, and one is in water.

I wanted to know more about the pelican, and, as if some one waved a magic wand, while I am in the lobby, the concierge shows me an article written on the local brown pelican. I knew they were big, but did not know they are among the largest birds in the world. The brown pelican at Virginia Beach has a wing-span of up to seven and one half feet. Plunge from 60 to 70 feet as she spies fish to eat. The air sacs in her breast cushion the blow of crashing full speed into the water. The birds' unique skin pouch is similar to a fishing net. They can scoop up a gallon or two of water along with one or several fish. The water drains from their pouch as they carry their catch in their mouth, not the pouch. They also use their pouch to cool off by pulsating it. Truly a wonder is the pelican.

I decided to connect with the pelicans in hopes they would have something to share with us.

It is late evening; I find the pelicans in my mind's eye south of our hotel down the beach, tucked into a cove and settling in for the night.

An older pelican comes forward. He says, *"Many, many years ago there were no pelicans in this area."* Pelican says their population increased, then decreased, and now is increasing once again. When there are few pelicans, some people see this as bad; others may see it as good. He explains, *"In the past, some local fishermen and residents thought we were a nuisance, now people enjoy our presence.*

Elder pelican says, *"Up or down, good or bad, it is what it is. There is always change. Make the most of whatever 'it' is. We do. We ride the currents on the ocean and we ride the currents of time."*

I investigated the pelican's increase and decrease of population through articles, and interviewed people who have researched and documented the history of the pelicans. To summarize: before the 1970s there were many pelicans on the south eastern Atlantic coast. Unfortunately, in the 1970s countless pelicans died from the chemical DDT. Once the brown pelican started to repopulate, a few migrated to Virginia Beach in the mid 1980s. Today, the pelican population there is strong and growing.

DDT cost the lives of many. Mr. Pelican, forgive us. Thankfully, nature is resilient, if we humans don't get in the way. May we hope to ride the air currents, or should I say life, as gracefully and joyfully as the pelican.

~~~~~~~~~~~~~~•••~~~~~~~~~~~~~

Simultaneous Conversations

During communications I may have two or more conversations going on simultaneously, the person I am listening to and the animal I am communicating with. Often
~~~~~~~~~~~~~~

other animals chime in, living or deceased. I also have my own thoughts swimming around in my head, plus my spiritual guides which come at times to help, as well. This means mentally receiving, understanding, and remembering several conversations. I keep a notebook close by, in which to write key words to give me reminders of whatever I cannot express because I am in conversation about something else.

There are also times when I receive a large assortment of information all at once from one source. It can be tricky learning to share the information in a way that makes sense to the person because it comes jumbled together. I have to stop myself, regroup the information and express it in an orderly way so that my client understands. I feel like a juggler at times. Goodness! Writing about what I do is actually more exhausting than managing everything in my head at one time, which somehow comes naturally to me. My motto is, do the best you can and pray for a good memory!

Because I am a detail person, I fine tune and automatically look deeper for more information. I realized after writing this segment, I might improve my communications by not being so intent on every bit of information all of the time. I have been known to get frustrated when I want more details or want a magic button to solve a problem. Frustration, if not handled properly, can hinder a communication. That is when I have to sit back and reassess how I am working with the animal and person or simply move on. Many times what I am trying to accomplish in the communication comes later when I understand another facet of the situation I am working on. Then, I at last understand. It is like finding the missing piece to a puzzle. The picture is complete.

19

L.B. the Accountant

"The smallest feline is a masterpiece."

~Leonardo Da Vince

Moving, new job, condo to be sold, and new home to be bought: all to be done in four months, more than my friend Libby wanted to contend with. In the midst of all this, on Libby's birthday a deserted injured kitten in need of surgery appeared near her home. Libby looked at this little ball of black and white fur as a birthday gift from God. Veterinary bills were not in her budget, but somehow Libby was determined to help the injured kitten. And she did, with perseverance and trust. The vet was generous with his services, as were neighbors who helped with expenses. A community came together for one hurting, homeless little kitty named Little Bit.

Little Bit repaid Libby's good deed in a manner which surprised us all. During a communication, the advice of a wise accountant came through this little cat. Libby was determined to put her home on the market at a low price in order to sell it quickly. Little Bit was convinced Libby's condo would sell for $8,000 more, a price which was out of Libby's comfort range. She needed to sell quickly and was afraid a high price would delay a deal. A discussion took place between Little Bit and Libby, with my facilitation, with an agreement of selling for $4,000 more than her original price. Libby sold the condo at that price! I later asked Libby if she could have sold it for more; she was silent for a second and then under her breath said, "My home sold quickly, so I probably could have."

Little Bit was not giving up his accounting job. Libby had a dream of living in a single-family home, preferably on the water, yet in her heart she felt her dream home was out of the question because of the high cost of living where she was relocating. Little Bit encouraged Libby not to give up on her dreams. Like magic, her real estate agent found such a home close to her price range. Little Bit tried to persuade Libby into offering $6,000 less than the asking price. Again, Libby balked. Little Bit persisted, and with a little wheeling and dealing, Libby again saved $4,000. With help from her precious kitty and others, Libby purchased her home on the water. Little Bit saved Libby a total of $8,000. I now call Little Bit "L.B., the accountant."

My mind spiraled as I wondered what Little Bit would communicate next. I looked forward to L.B.'s message. I am usually surprised with the knowledge this little one shares.

L.B. has been waiting. He knows my thoughts have been about him.

I am sooo impressed with myself; I have heard you and Libby talk about my genius advice, yet I did not comprehend the total impact it had. Do you think anyone would like to pay for my services?

"When this book is published, we will find out, L.B."

People get stewed up over nothing. Expecting all will go wrong, this affects the natural flow of events. Some live as if difficulties have already happened. The body becomes tense, sleepless nights, worry, worry, worry. Follow your common sense and instincts. Know your circumstances will work out, and when you treat life this way you receive the bounty you ask for and more.

Simply, keep it simple.

When one is through the day, give thanks to all, not forgetting oneself.

Seeing is clearer when one keeps one's vision clear of outside, non-relevant issues. Getting upset over situations that have not occurred is wasted energy. It has nothing to do with adding and subtracting.

Simplify one's thoughts when going through seemingly difficult or tedious situations. The human mind becomes mottled, creating situations which do not take place, yet one acts emotionally and physically like they have. Work a plan moving through your goal, trust and hold a mental state of all is well and will be. If the plan changes, continue to hold on to that faith—all is well and will be. If life throws more curves, work the plan, as all is well and will be.

L.B. quickly goes back to his kitty business, playing and enjoying being a healthy kitten.

~~~~~~~~~~~~~~~•••~~~~~~~~~~~~~

Written Information

Being telepathic is not entirely the answer to solutions with animals. Education helps as well.
~~~~~~~~~~~~~~~

There are many products for animals on the market. To know them all, is impossible. Describing an unfamiliar image an animal is giving me can be difficult to explain to her person. A Tennessee Walking horse, Melody, was asking for a specific bit. It was difficult for me to describe which bit Melody wanted. As hard as I tried, her person, Becky, could not relate to my description. After going through her tack room and catalogs, Becky fortunately was able to find a bit similar to my description. Shortly afterwards Becky gave me several catalogues that featured not only bits but other horse products. These pictures were most appreciated. I now had a frame of reference to call specific items by their correct names.

When in a communication where a client does not relate to her lost animal's surroundings or directions of where he is, an Internet map site can improve the success of finding them. As the client and I are on the phone looking at our computers with the same Internet map site giving visuals of terrain and road names, we can understand directions and surroundings.

I zoom in for a closer visual where the animal was last seen and combine my instinct and guidance from the animal, fine tuning directions for my worried client. A missing dog showed me he was near a yellowish, three-story structure. The best I could relate to in my understanding, being a farm girl, was a wide silo. The map showed it was a small dam. This information gave the person a focus on where to look for her lost animal. When my clients went to the dam area, a local man said he had seen the dog that day. But the dog was not in sight when they arrived. This was one of those cases when the dog was not ready to go home. He was having fun with his new-found freedom.

When an animal describes a tree in a forest or a town home in a residential development, the differences can be difficult to point out. At times like this I go to an area on the map site and look over the property with my mind's eye. This is called remote viewing. Once I have found a defined area, I combine this information and what I receive through the animals' eyes, ears and nose for details that will distinguish a specific spot. The animal may see a flower pot with yellow flowers on the steps of a town home, hear children playing, or smell burgers cooking on an outside grill. Some believe animals do not see colors. Whether they do or not, when I look through an animal's eyes, I see colors.

In dealing with lost animals, the more quickly the client calls, the better the odds are in finding her animal. That is, if the animal wants to be found. One example is shown in chapter 23 in the second segment called Divinely Orchestrated: A Jack Russell terrier ran away from home and would not tell me where she was hiding.

I wish I had utilized Google Map and other sites earlier in my career. Perhaps the animals I missed would have been found.

The Encyclopedia of Horses & Ponies and other books referencing cats and dogs, by Tamsin Pickerel, are books I came across in my earlier years as a communicator. They have been invaluable, with pictures and information about breeds I am not familiar with. Anatomy charts in my books and other charts I have obtained have helped give specifics for a better understanding of what or where the animal's problem is.

I have acquired charts that show different colors and markings of animals. When a client says her horse has an eel stripe, I for one, would be perplexed. I associate eels with the ocean. Through my horse book, I discovered an eel stripe is a black or dark brown stripe that extends from the withers along the backbone and down into the tail. The proper name can give better understanding to my client and to me. There are many kinds of critters, and to memorize all of their colors, markings and breeds would be overwhelming.

Many times I simply know I am connected to the correct animal when working over the phone without a picture. I sense the energy of the animal I am in communication with and it feels correct. I do not go through the process of comparing my description of the animal with the client's description. Liver colored, or pips, which are spots above a dog's eyes, I do not need to know what these words mean. I just need to know that I know. All the reference books in the world are not necessary. What is necessary is that my client believes I have the correct animal. However, correct descriptions are available, if needed.

20

Discerning Discipline

"A dog gladly admits the superiority of his master over himself, accepts his judgment as final but, contrary to what dog lovers believe, he does not consider him as a slave. His submission is voluntary, and he expects his own small rights to be respected."

~Alex Munthe

Horatio is a young French bulldog. He lives in a small neighborhood and roams where he pleases. Horatio's mind goes in many directions at once. When I first contacted with him, he could not decide if he should chase the geese, find Mr. Turtle who would not come out to play, pester workers building a house down the road, or check out his neighbor in hopes their granddaughters will be visiting. The wheels in his mind turn constantly!

I asked if he had learned something of importance in his youth that he would like to share.

Horatio began:

I came here to learn about discipline. What does it do for you? I enjoy exploring my neighborhood. When my people call me home, I think about what I want to do. Is it better to play because a neighbor child or adult is enjoying my company? Should I visit the geese who are taking over someone's yard? Perhaps checking on Turtle who tries to hide from me should be my next mission. Or is it best to head home?

What I am learning is to discern all I do. Some decisions that seem logically right are not. I do what feels good; this is my discipline.

Horatio then ran off to play!

Horatio makes his decisions in a manner that is different from many adult humans, perhaps more in tune with human children. We have been taught to move through life rationally. Horatio listens to his heart, his feelings. If it feels good, he will do it. If not, he won't. When we make decisions in this manner, we are in tune with our inner guidance, which at times conflicts with the way we have been conditioned. Trust and have faith in doing what feels good. Give it a try.

~~~~~~~~~~~~•••~~~~~~~~~~~~

Sensitive Information

There will be times when I receive information I don't fully understand, yet this information makes a great impact on the people I am giving it to.
~~~~~~~~~~~~

I have learned to respect both the first immediate thoughts I receive and also the bits of information that briefly come to mind. These gut feelings, faint fleeting words or insights can be the most accurate—believe in what you receive. Have you jumped up from your favorite chair to give your dog a bone or take him on a walk? Don't think it was your own idea!

I was once in a relaxed atmosphere while visiting with a group of ladies I had recently met. They could not resist asking questions about their animals when they discovered I was an animal communicator. As I answered, I spontaneously expressed what one dog asked her person: *When are you going to see the new man you're having an affair with?* I did not know about this lady's personal life; fortunately, she was relieved "the cat was out of the bag" and she could now share this information with her friends, which, actually, was not a surprise to them! They knew she was ending a difficult marriage. Perhaps her dog did, indeed, know what was best for her person.

On another occasion, I was giving a communication for two gentlemen and their dogs. The mother of one of these fellows came to visit from Florida with her Lhasa Apso dog. Her son asked if she had any questions for her dog. Immediately she said, "No, I am afraid of what she might say!" At that moment her little dog walked over to my feet and plopped down on them. The two men looked at each other and said, "OK, we will ask her." They asked general questions, then asked if the dog had anything to say to them. Still sitting on my feet the little dog looked over to her person, then back to the two men. I then relayed a message she wanted the two men to know.

In a concerned voice the dog said, *She drinks more in Florida.* The little dog walked over to her person who picked her up and said, "I do not!" and left the room. I looked at the two men who were eyeing each other. After a short pause, one said to the other, "I believe the dog!" My first thought was, Florida is hot so they drink more fluids. I did not know Mother had a drinking problem.

I may not always know the meaning behind some of the information I receive, but I always hope for good to come from these situations.

Animal communications have impacted people and critters in many ways. But some are to the extreme. Beth worked for Homeland Security in the White House. After the bombing of the Twin Towers and plane crash at the Pentagon on September the eleventh, Beth was beyond stressed. Her health was, according to her dog Jack, being compromised. In our communication Jack kept repeating, "go on vacation." I kept hearing it, so I kept saying it. Repeating the message over and over again was annoying. At one point I apologized to Beth, yet I had to stay true to what I was receiving. I was drawn to ask her what she really wanted to do in life. Beth wanted to work with animals in some manner, but she was not sure how. She thought, perhaps, rescuing dogs or an animal sanctuary. Her mind kept trying to find what it would be. She then shared that her favorite animal was the monkey. Unusual, I thought. And then Jack began again, go on vacation, go on vacation.

One year later Beth called. She announced that she did go on vacation. She and her brother went on a fabulous trip to Puerto Rico. Both fell in love with the area and bought property while visiting. Her property is on the top of a mountain with a panoramic view of the ocean, and…. monkeys migrate on her property in front of her house every morning and evening. It gets better yet—her brother met a man who gave them a large grant to help animals in Puerto Rico. I almost went into shock hearing her news. I could not make a story up like this one, and I have a vivid imagination.

Another communication creating change was with Sue and her tiny Chihuahua, Pepsi. Pepsi's main focus was sharing he was cold when outside; he needed a special coat. Sue could not find a wrap in the stores that would fit him. Sue called six months later. She had quit her job and had started manufacturing animal clothing.

I have learned, when annoyed, don't be! What seems small can be BIG!

21

Slow But Wise

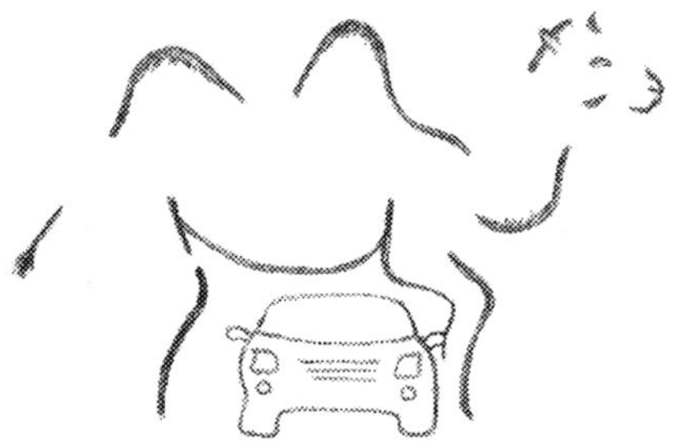

"Never does nature say one thing and wisdom another."

~Juvenal, Satires

We felt like three little kids anxious for adventure. LeAndra Shepherd's brilliant idea created the day: she, my husband, John, and I headed out for Safari Park near Natural Bridge, Virginia. Upon arrival, we purchased tubs of feed for the animals and were given the rules of the park. With cameras in hand and windows down, we drove slowly into the park. We had no idea what to expect from what we assumed about wild life. Like a magnet they came, llamas, emus, ostriches, zebras, and camels. Heads large and small poked into the windows for food. The three of us inside the car burst into screams and laughter, flailing our hands about to shoo them away. Wild, timid animals? I think not. They knew the routine well—cars and people represent food. Without delay we raised all windows. Now large brown eyes peered through the windows. The animals looked as if we had wronged them.

A large Asian camel standing in front of our car prevented us from moving forward. He stared at us saying, *I know you have food. I will not move until a bucket of food emerges from your window.*

Windows up, and now feeling safe within the car, John and I turned to each other; however, we did not see each other. A massive brown camel's head with big nostrils and lips moving about in search of food now encompassed the middle of the front seat. We had forgotten to close the sunroof! Pandemonium erupted once again with our backs pressed against the car door window. Our crazy antics did not bother Mr. Camel one bit; he had adapted to this human behavior. In fact, I felt he enjoyed the commotion he had created. With no food available, Mr. Camel slowly withdrew his big furry head from the sunroof. The surprise of seeing the camel created a reaction from me I wish had been different. I realized I had missed an opportunity to enjoy this magnificent animal. I was saddened he was gone.

After adjusting to the animals' we learned to enjoy their every move. Now composed, we realized they were safe, and we invited them into the car, well, just their heads. An American bison put his big burly head into the car window for food. My lap was all bison, we were face-to-face. I rubbed his forehead. He seemed to like it. Most likely he was enjoying the food more. For those who have never petted a bison, their hair is wiry. If we had opened the car door, critters would have climbed in. That was not going to happen, as it is against the park rules!

Once our drive-through journey ended, we piled out of the car to stretch our legs. The large Asian camel that invited himself through our sunroof now stood next to a fence, not far from where we'd parked. I sensed his neck itched and would appreciate a good scratching. As I walked towards him, I found it interesting he did not leave to get food from a car that had just entered the park.

Although I may have a sense of an animal's demeanor, it is always wise to be careful, especially around wild animals. Fortunately Mr. Camel was gentle. He leaned towards me as I scratched his huge, thick neck. I loved being in his presence. I had a feeling of being safe, loved and yet powerful. I wanted to feel like this, forever.

I took Mr. Camel's actions as a cue for a conversation. I decided to wait until I had my laptop to type his words. I did not want to miss one thought.

Once home, after we'd washed animal slobbers from the car and vacuumed pellets of animal food from every corner of the interior, I connected with Mr. Camel. He spoke in an extremely slow—and I mean *extremely* slow—methodical manner. For once my typing could keep up with the message.

You forgot I am not only gentle and kind, I am patient, too. People are most humorous. A new car to the safari is always fun. The young ones don't know the tricks of the trade! They need to learn from us old wise two-humpers. Been around for a long time, like some of the others here. All we want is a good meal, a place to rest, to be loved and cared for.

It is not healthy for animals to get bored in captivity; thanks to people like you three, that will never happen to me.

"It was our pleasure to feed and entertain you. Would you like to entertain us with some words of wisdom?"

Life goes on; make the best of it. When you give, you get back. Life can be a bowl of candy, or camel feed, if you want it to be. When mosquitoes fly around you, swat 'em, no need to put up with 'em. Soak in cooling water when it is hot. When your feet get sore, quit standing. If you get tired, rest. Don't blame your problems on others. If it is windy, enjoy the breeze. If you need a change, change. When in a foreign country, act foreign. If it rains, enjoy it, or get out of it. If others annoy ya, ignore them, or leave. If you're hungry, eat.

If you overeat, don't. Forget the shoes, feel the earth. Don't look in the mirror, look at others. When you're suffering, heal yourself. Understand yourself first, then others. Run, don't crawl, when you know you should be doing a great deed. When the day seems long, create excitement! Happiness is a figment of your imagination, so imagine. When you're done speaking your mind, stop.

"Thank you for your wise words, Mr. Camel."

Hope to see you again with a bucket of feed at the sunroof. Walk in peace.

~~~~~~~~~~~~~~~•••~~~~~~~~~~~~~

Positive Direction

Giving animals detailed information helps an animal understand the reason behind a behavior asked of them. Take the example of a large dog that jumps on every one who comes through the front door. I would send the dog specific feelings showing how the person would feel being forced upon, hurt, or how the person would not like animals putting their paws on their clothing. I would explain further to the dog why people do not like this behavior so the dog may understand. Many times this imaging alone takes care of the problem, yet I always encourage positive training techniques from a dog trainer or book to help reinforce the behavior you want.

A cat who climbs the screens and rips them causes inconvenience, time, money and frustration to those living in the house. I would explain to the cat why people do not like this behavior as well as listen to why he is climbing the screens. Sometimes there is an important message to the person. I then show him, through my thoughts, a cat tree or something else provided by his person as a substitute for him to climb on. I reinforce these images with really, really
~~~~~~~~~~~~~~~

happy feelings as I envision him climbing on the cat tree or substitute. This process has proven to solve many problems.

It is helpful when we hold in our mind what we want our animal to do. When we think of what we don't want animals to do, whether we are at home, work or on vacation, we can actually influence them. When speaking to a cat and she hears *don't jump on the counter,* the cat picks up on the thought—*counter*— and she is attracted to the counter. In your mind, hold pictures of your animal on the floor or another acceptable place.

22

The Monkey Dance

"Re-examine all you have been told….Dismiss what insults your soul."

~Walt Whitman

At a Safari Park in Virginia, monkeys glide from one end of their large outside cage to the other. Great acrobats they are, bodies agile, jumping, swinging, and climbing throughout their cage. Monkeys' antics can be fascinating. Their tongues and lips move in all sorts of directions, their vocal cords create high-pitched sounds, and their bodies move freely.

Such coordination! What fun it would be to move like a monkey.

Trying to capture a particular outspoken monkey on camera was impossible. His head, eyes, and body language spoke to us the best he could, saying— *I see, smell, and want your popcorn!*

Several months later, Monkey powerfully returned to my thoughts. In my mind I could see him hanging from his wire cage. He looked at me with his big round eyes and then with a leap swung from one part of his cage to another, the same as when I'd visited him at Safari Park.

I was almost finished with my communications for this book and was not going to approach Monkey. However, he was a persistent rascal.

It has been cool and they have made provisions for us to stay warm through the winter months. Are you coming to see me this spring? I feel the excitement inside you wanting to share this festival of animals where I live with others. It is great fun.

"You are so right, I am counting the days until your home is open to the public again."

OH, GOOD, please bring your popcorn.

"The keepers are concerned that you eat healthy foods, but I will see what I can do."

Did you know the children understand us the best?

"I have thought so."

They have not forgotten, the little ones. They see differently than the adults. After a while adults forget. It is truly the adults who have forgotten to learn from the children. It would bring back warmth to both their lives.

Movement is important for my way of life; movement is important for your way of life. Chairs are an excuse not to use your muscles. Lazy types you are. Movement helps bring the truth in and the old dark stuff out. It is called freeing up. Jump up and down a few times, swing your arms like a monkey. Make odd sounds you are not used to making and see what happens. Do this daily. See what happens.

Vibration, sound, movement, wonderful. You might be called insane, yet it keeps the sanity.

Sanity, isn't that an interesting subject. One lives in Africa, one lives in New York City, one lives in China, one lives in Afghanistan, one lives in the Australian outback. They all live differently. Where you sit, would you say they all live in a sane manner? Do not judge how people or animals live or act. Perhaps you are being judged insane by others. Understand the differences, or not. Just accept there are many ways.

You are the way you are for a reason. Accept it and live it fully, or change it if you wish for something different. Move freely; restricting movements limit possibilities.

If you think I am in a cage, perhaps you should look at yourselves; you created your own. I am freer than many of you.

Humm…, well, Mr. Monkey, I will give the monkey dance a try, but I will close the blinds when I do so.

A few days later I gave the monkey dance a try—very awkwardly at first. Yet, wow, once I got into this unusual behavior, it was quite invigorating and fun; it was freeing. The mucky muck, as I call it, was gone. Sometimes we do not realize our bodies are holding onto energy that is weighing us down. Do the monkey dance!

~~~~~~~~~~~~~•••~~~~~~~~~~~~~

Misunderstood

At times our wonderful companions just will not behave. A little dog named Hardy was kept separated from his person in another room because he was snapping at her and others. Hardy barked incessantly because he wanted to be close to his person. After four years of loving companionship, both of
~~~~~~~~~~~~~

them found this separation difficult. The dog trainer, a dog psychologist, a vet, and even the neighbors tried to help.

This person had done everything she could to help her canine friend. Now it was my turn. Hardy communicated that he was misunderstood. The guidance given by other people was to discipline him, but when I connected with Hardy he showed me what he was feeling. I experienced a sharp pain, in my upper neck and into my head. When a hand came close to this area on the dog he usually snapped at it. Because the painful area was where people petted him or placed his leash, he snapped quite often.

Discerning how my neck was feeling, I felt as if his vertebrae were out of alignment, perhaps pinching a nerve. After our communication, the person made an appointment with a veterinarian for a thorough examination. Fortunately, the vet was also an animal chiropractor. The vet found a severe misalignment in Hardy's upper neck vertebrae.

I have learned that no matter how convincing a person's explanation is regarding a critter's problem, the explanation might not hold true. In this case Hardy's problem was a health issue, not a discipline problem which his person and others had presumed, and medical attention was needed.

23

Who Am I?

"My country is the world and my religion is to do good."

~Thomas Paine

At the end of our journey through Safari Park, I watched a baby zebra in the distance next to her mother. She stared intently, observing us as we petted and fed a variety of animals. I wondered what else was going on in her head.

Once home, I connected in thought and wondered what an innocent baby zebra would have to say. I could see her in my mind's eye. She was staring at me again, watching, just as she did at the park. I explained to her who I was. She seemed confused.

Baby Zebra began to speak:

I don't know if I should talk to you. You're a stranger. I feel strange enough being me! I don't know who I am and why I am here.

"I have had the same feelings in my life. Would you like to share your confusion?"

My mother explained to me that this land we are on is not our homeland. She has told me stories of my original land, its beauty and how it was a great place to live. She says it has changed, as I have changed from those who lived before me. I should not forget who I am, and should learn to be at peace with this land. I feel as if . . . . life is not black and white; there are a lot of gray areas I do not understand. I am two different zebras—the one of my past zebra relatives, and the one I am now. How do I fit in?

"You have the same feelings many people have. Your mother is very wise. Perhaps she can help."

Mother Zebra has been listening intently to her baby. She understands what her little one is going through, for it was her mother who shared this same information with her.

Mother Zebra made herself present to me. Her energy is of such greatness; I feel a lump in my throat, and awe. Mother Zebra began to share what she learned from her mother.

We all came from different places and traveled in many ways to fulfill life's purposes. A most important time was when we remembered we were all great. All will remember, no matter what color, country, or by which mother or father you came into this world. The most important thing in this life is to reclaim the magnitude of who we can be. My baby can reclaim it here at the safari, in your backyard, or in the great land she came from. She is special; I know it, and when she does understand the depth of who she is she will help others understand. This can happen without knowing that it is taking place. It simply will begin. My baby is my successor to help others as I have. Those that leave this park are not the same as when they came. Some know on a grand scale, others small. A spark is lit no matter how big. We have made a difference. It helps to see the spark in us, the light we are, and together our sparks unite, becoming bigger together. Yes, dear ones, we are one.

Wherever you are, claim your own power, wisdom, joy, and feel your beauty. Do not blame circumstances that are around you for your unhappiness. You created the circumstances, blame yourself. Claim and create the life you want. Go to nature; we will help you remember how.

There is much going on with spiritual evolution, as well as involution—returning to our former condition. We are actually going back, remembering—remembering that there was once a great peace in our hearts and we are claiming it again. African ones, remember your peace, for great happiness awaits you. You have a great job—to carry peace in your hearts. It will boost this planet into paradise; you will be in such awe, some will find it uncomfortable at first. Adjust, enjoy, marvel at, and relish in the experience.

People with hard hearts of pain, let go of your burdens; you are the ones to help create the new heaven on earth. It is your journey on this earth to find the peace inside of you. You are the great ones.

These are powerful words; remember them.

Mother Zebra reminded me to move on with my process in life and to share her words with others. I commit once again to share the wisdom of the animal kingdom.

~~~~~~~~~~~~~•••~~~~~~~~~~~~~

Divinely Orchestrated

Many times the animals we choose, or who choose us, reflect our own personalities—for better or for worse. Critters who display non-stop love, attention, and tenderness may be reflecting the same love and tenderness of their persons. These animals are great blessings, particularly when
~~~~~~~~~~~~~

their person is facing difficult times. Likewise, overly-aggressive animals may be responding to hateful, fearful, or combative behavior of their person. At times, their behavior reflects the need of discipline or boundaries in that person's life as well as needing discipline and boundaries in the animal's life. It is often the case that when we observe our animals we see aspects of ourselves.

Sadie and Jack are Jack Russell terriers who live with a family of four. Pam, the family's mother, trained the two dogs who have been on numerous T.V. advertisements. Her training and discipline did not seem to make a difference, however, when Sadie attacked Jack for what seemed no apparent reason. Pam remembered our conversation on how animals reflect our own moods. Putting two and two together, she began to see the pattern of Sadie reflecting the family situation by attacking Jack when family arguments occurred. Pam thought it best to find another home for Sadie since she was causing even more stress within the family when she fought with Jack. She asked if I would like to take Sadie. What an offer! This was one of the cutest, best-trained dogs I knew. It was tempting, yet this dedicated little one said, *No way*—she had unfinished business with her family. What loyalty!

A frantic call came several weeks later. Sadie had run away—out the door, through the back yard, and over the fence while the family was arguing. I connected with Little Miss Runaway—she showed me places she had been romping in the woods behind her back yard. Her family found these places I described not far from their home, yet there was no Sadie. Sadie usually communicates like a pro, but today communication was quite difficult. Was she hiding from me, too? Pam and I both had a gut feeling Sadie was safe, yet we really wanted to see her two big dark eyes up close for validation. One clear message Sadie did give me: *If I do come home, and they argue, I will run away again.* Sadie also gave suggestions on how the family could handle their family feuds in a more productive manner—*apologize for hurtful words—be true to your feelings—express them calmly—resolve your differences.*

During the time Sadie was gone, her family had time to reflect and talk about how they were going to manage their disagreements. Sadie, on the other hand, was having a good time. During her family crises, she had found a fun family with two little girls to take care of her. This family called the local animal shelter to report Little Miss Runaway. Pam had reported Sadie missing to the same shelter, but when she was given the phone number of the people that had Sadie, either the shelter gave her the wrong number or she wrote it down wrong. A few days later Pam decided to call the shelter again. This time she had the correct number. Sadie now had her ticket home—with perfect timing. Because of the incorrect phone number, the family was given more time to worry about Sadie and take her advice seriously. If Sadie had come home earlier, she would not have gotten the results she wanted. But this was not the end of the story.

A few weeks later there was another family feud, and Sadie was true to her promise—out the door, over the fence and off she ran. Fortunately, Sadie was found along the side of the road by a truck driver and returned home. The family once again looked at what they were doing to each other and made corrections.

The oldest son had become worried about Sadie's reactions and would quickly find Sadie and hold onto her when a family feud was about to erupt. The parents noticed the son's actions, which also influenced handling family matters in a calmer manner. There was more work to be done within the family dynamics, but the wheels had started turning in a healthier direction—instigated by a little Jack Russell terrier.

I love this example of what animals will do to support us and themselves. I would call this adventure divinely orchestrated! In a similar situation, a cat named Bigsby said, *I love them so much I will do anything to help my family.*

24

Be Aware with Care

"Divine Spirit speaks to us through its creatures and through nature."

~Sir Harold Klemp

Mornings are glorious for John and me. We start our day watching a golden-red sun slowly rise over the mountains reflecting on Smith Mountain Lake. We leisurely sip a hot drink on our porch as the day comes alive. The crows start their chatter. Soon a variety of birds, squirrels, and rabbits join us to feed on seeds and nuts scattered on the ground close to where we sit. Some are bold enough to play under our chairs.

A young rabbit had been eating corn off our porch for several weeks. He was quite comfortable sharing this space with us. We looked forward to seeing him every morning, and I believe he felt the same. He emanated a sweet, yet wise nature. At times when visiting human friends shared this space, Bunny would sit quietly a few feet away and stare at them with his big, soft, brown eyes. Bunny and I made a good team setting the visitor up for this moment.

Once Bunny came bouncing up to a friend and me, stopping three feet away from where we sat. He stared at my friend for quite a while until she looked at me and said, "What does he want?"

I asked Bunny this question as he continued looking at her. Bunny said, *"Tell her she worries too much about small things. She puts everything she feels she needs to do in one big ball as if she has to do it all at once. Relax, enjoy what you do as it needs to be done."*

On another occasion, Bunny advised a gentleman to enjoy life; his worries were needless. He told a young lady the reason she took care of her dog in special ways was that she needed the same thing in her life. She deserved to be treated special, too. Tears came to her eyes.

An older, depressed lady, who had never experienced an animal companion, believed animals were not capable of wisdom or emotions. Bunny gave her this message: *We love you unconditionally, and when you have an animal companion and realize they are part of God as you are too, your eyes will see a bigger picture. We are closer to God than many people. When you become closer to God, and see God in you, you will discover we are all God's. God is everywhere. I am clear that everywhere means everywhere. That does not exclude animals.*

I asked Bunny for insights to share with those who read this book, and he jumped at the opportunity.

You humans need to be careful in what you do to yourselves. I see more and more woods being cut down. You need the woods as much as we do. What you don't realize is, we animals are learning to adapt to your ways more than you are. We still have more contact with nature, which helps keep us balanced. Some do not know what being with nature is anymore; some, not a clue. How sad!

"Thank you, Bunny, I appreciate your wise words. With so much wooded area destroyed, I have been concerned for bunnies and other wildlife. I never realized you might be concerned for us. Would you mind if I take your picture?"

You may, if you put my special food out. I will pose for you by the flowers.

He knew I loved the colorful flowers on our porch—and obviously he knew how to get what he wanted.

"I accept. Would you like to give a message intended for children?" I think Bunny put this thought into my head. He is a tricky one!

OOOHH, YYEESS!
Hop through life without a care
Not aware
You might hop smack into a rock
So, be aware
With great care
Life will be filled with bunny springs
Loving adventures filled with blessings
A bunny is wise, so take this advice in your lives

Bunny was very pleased with his poem, and so was I.

The next day, I put Bunny's special seeds on our porch for him. Bunny appeared within minutes excited about his treat. I grabbed my camera. As I started to point and focus at Bunny, I wondered about our agreement, and at that point he hopped away! I put my camera down and to my amazement, he hopped in front of our flowers. I froze and watched him, his pose perfect, head up high, body straight, looking directly at me with multi-colored flowers all around his brown, handsome body. For a short while he looked at me as if he were smiling, then off he hopped. I missed his perfect pose for the camera, yet in that moment I was enjoying it so much it did not matter. That moment will always be with me.

Bunny told me as I typed: *Bunny rabbits do not lie. We are truthful.*

~~~~~~~~~~~~~••••~~~~~~~~~~~~~

123

Animal Weather Predictions

Early one winter, I started to see a pattern after several communications with local animals. Gertrude, an elderly turkey, asked for more bedding. Several chickens asked for extra straw for bedding, and wanted bales of straw placed around the walls of their chicken house. Two horses who slept in a partially open shed requested more wood shavings, giving me the image of them curled up in it for warmth. Ten days later, we had one of our coldest weeks in several years.

Weather has become a popular topic around the world. Crazy, unpredictable hurricanes, floods, mudslides, fires, and earthquakes are affecting our lives. By paying more attention to animal behavior, and fine-tuning our own natural instincts, we can improve our lives in many ways—perhaps—save lives.
~~~~~~~~~~~~~

25

Making Sense

"If we can learn to become more aware of and attuned to coincidences, more cognizant of their significance, then we will evolve to a higher state of being."

~Yitta Halberstam

Cujo is a seventeen-year-old golden lab who loves to high-five with his paw. Cujo's human companion manages a restaurant and deals with a myriad of tasks. In our first communication, Cujo stated he was concerned about the many business and personal decisions his person makes. When I approached Cujo a second time, for a contribution to this book, he believed he had nothing of value to share. I encouraged him to give it a try. Cujo thought a while, then began:

It is frustrating when people perceive my physical movements as the only way to understand me. People see us and believe they know what we want. There are some people who treat other people similar to this—they are usually not the expressive type. I'll call it a communication shortage.

I am learning to express myself differently. Speaking words is limiting. If more people used thought with feelings, pictures, and other forms of communication, we would understand each other incredibly better.

With that said, I am willing to share of myself.

When I sniff the ground and "put my attention" to what is around me, I receive a variety of information from all my senses. As I smell a scent, I know who it is. I feel the soil if moist, dry, cold or warm. I hear bugs, wind, and whispers. I can sense feelings, moods, and personalities of others. A whole world of information can be accessed. My words to you are this: Be aware of all aspects of your surroundings wherever you are. A change in people's behavior, a schedule not working, how you live your life, or even the placement of furniture or equipment. If you're not happy with these aspects of life, or others I have not mentioned, take action; change it so life flows smoothly once again. Change is growth. These little things we pick up on early can prevent large problems later.

Some of you won't acknowledge you have these senses, but we all do! Use them to understand the warnings and solutions. Tune in, take notice, and please don't ignore what you receive.

Doesn't this make sense?

High-five.

"High-five back to you, Cujo."

~~~~~~~~~~~~~•••~~~~~~~~~~~~

Animal Personalities

Animals have different personalities. Herbie, an iguana I communicate with, talks like a staunch Englishman. I want to put a top hat on his head, hand him a cane, and perhaps some wing-tipped shoes. A python named Jake has the personality of a hard-core Texan—boots and a cowboy hat fit his temperament. A matronly mare, Perrier, would be dressed in an old fashioned apron, hair pulled up on her head, and—in her few minutes of spare time—seated in her rocker on the front porch where she would give advice to anyone who passes by. It is fun portraying animals' personalities to their people, and most people relate to the images.
~~~~~~~~~~~~~

26

Follow Your Dreams

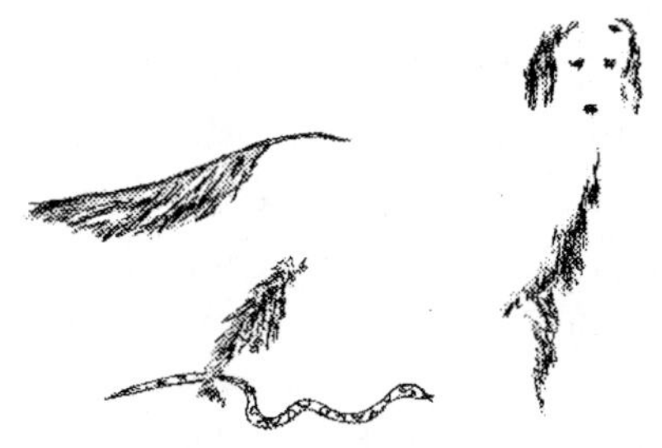

"When nature has work to be done, she creates a genius to do it."

~Ralph Waldo Emerson

Nancy has had many of her own communications with her six-year old Irish setter, Tommy. She could tell by the very intense look in Tommy's eyes that he had an important message for her, yet she was experiencing a problem connecting with him. Sometimes when communicators are excessively emotional with their animals, they have difficulties understanding the telepathic information correctly. Consequently, they often ask another communicator for help. That's when I entered the picture.

During my conversation with Tommy, he shared personal insights about his loving companion's life. Nancy taught advanced horseback riding and was a horse trainer, training fifteen horses that are talented enough for international competition. Two horses are being considered by the Olympic selection committee. Tommy encouraged her to tell her equestrian students about communications she was having with their horses during their classes. This would give the students added insights to enhance their riding abilities. They could have two teachers at the same time— what a combination! The communication would be fun, informative and—when coming from the animal—could sometimes be understood on a deeper level, thus enhancing the teaching even more. This information would take her teaching to a new level that her competitors did not have.

Nancy was quiet after I shared this information with her. She wondered if she should or not. Sharing her gift would be out of her comfort zone, not everyone accepts or believes in animal communication. In her heart, she wanted to take Tommy's advice. But, she could not bring herself to do so. Perhaps Nancy will when she becomes more confident.

My thoughts go to Tommy.

"Hi, Tommy, were you happy with your communication?"

Yes, mission accomplished. Didn't realize I made an impression on you.

"If you would share some of your wisdom, Tommy, I would greatly appreciate it."

Simple, love to! Keep yourself close to what you want in life or it sneaks away like a snake.

"Is that all you have to say?"

That's not enough?

"I expected more. You expressed yourself with lengthy, detailed answers to Nancy.

Details! You humans, you make life so complicated. What do you want details on, snakes or wants of life?

"Wants of life."

What do you want? Do you truly know? Most of you do what other people tell you to do. Started when you were a baby. Parents think they are doing their best, been handed down from generation to generation.

Tommy stops talking, I wait.

Don't stop typing, Karen!

"You have to keep talking for me to type."

I have complete control here! What power it gives, I can say anything and you will write it down—that is, if you can quit making errors in your typing as I speak!

"Okay Tommy, that's a low blow. It took a lot of work and grit to get where I am. I must say with the persistence of you animals, I am doing the best I can. I am going through trying times learning how to use this computer and working hard on my first book. Give me a break!"

You're a perfect example, the snake did not get away. You have a vision and are holding on to it. That takes courage. You act on what you need to do. Doesn't it feel good to be in action doing what you enjoy and working with obstacles that once stopped you? I realize learning to use a computer and facing misspelled words and grammar mistakes are some of your insecurities, not to mention people and their reactions to you being an animal communicator. Insecurities have stopped you several times from pursuing a dream. Facing the music is important.

I used you to make my point!

People, don't let go of your dreams or you'll get caught in the quagmire of life. One day you may wake up and find, oops, it's too late. WAKE UP! Whose fault is it? Yours, slumbering people. Quit blaming everyone else, it's YOU you have to look at. YOU can do it, YOU have all it takes.

I have to repeat myself. I have found people don't understand or act unless repetition is enforced.

Tommy ends his communication with a final message: *I am at peace with myself. Are you? Follow your dreams.*

~~~~~~~~~~~~~•••~~~~~~~~~~~~~

Achilles' Heel

The best communicators have been known to call another communicator when needing to touch base with their own animals, especially when the person is stressed about their own animal. The person's stressful emotion with their animal kinks the hose through which information is received.

My worst problem when communicating is being tired. I tend to shut down when receiving information. Some people find specific foods or drinks affect their communications; a few common ones are caffeine, meat, or alcohol. Pay attention to what your Achilles' heel might be when it comes to communicating.
~~~~~~~~~~~~~

27

Growing Old

"Heaven goes by favor. If it went by merit, you would stay out and your dog would go in."

~Mark Twain

Dixie, an eighteen year-old yellow cocker spaniel, is thin and frail. I became concerned about Dixie when her family was going through a difficult divorce. Not only was Dixie sensitive to extreme stress in the family, but her needs were being overlooked. Dixie appeared to be giving up on life. During our last communication, she spoke of where she thought her people would want her to be buried.

Shortly after our conversation, Dixie's situation took an interesting turn.

The daughter in Dixie's family had been her original companion when both were younger. She had moved away and now had a daughter of her own. Both came to reclaim Dixie. They wanted to give Dixie the love and attention an old dog needed and deserved.

I wondered how Dixie was doing and decided to contact her.

I remember you. How are you doing?

"I am well, Dixie. Would you like to share your wisdom for a book I am writing?

In what way, lovely lady?

"Your opinion on any subject, anything of importance to you—it's your call."

What a privilege!

Dixie thought for a moment and then began:

Growing old snuck up on me. One day I realized small problems should not have been so troublesome when privileges I took for granted like walking, hearing, and seeing greatly diminished. I say to you, take good care of yourself, live each moment fully, and see its joys. When your body starts to give out, know the body isn't really you.

"Thank you, Dixie, what a precious dog you are. Your words are wise for all ages."

Approximately ten months after our communication, Dixie moved on to doggy heaven.

~~~~~~~~~~~~~••••~~~~~~~~~~~~~

Time to Die

Helping a person deal with a beloved animal that is ready to pass on can be rewarding. To know and understand the joy it brings an animal when she slips out of a hurting, old, tired
~~~~~~~~~~~~~

body can be an amazing experience for both animal and person. The process of exchanging loving words with understanding why their lives came together, helps the process tremendously. Once an animal has *moved out,* as an Irish setter, Willy, once described it to me, the spirit can be with its person anywhere, any time. I have spoken to many people who express their awareness of their animal's presence after death. Some can actually feel them, and some have seen their spirit.

With phone at ear, on hold, I waited to be interviewed on a radio talk show. The production assistant, a young lady named Jill, had prepped me on what was to take place, and then took the moment to engage me in a conversation about her deceased cat, Molly. While Jill was talking about Molly, Molly was also talking to me from the spirit realm at the same time. Molly explained to me that many times while Jill is seated at her work desk she feels as if she needs to brush something off her lower legs—that was Molly moving in a figure eight between Jill's legs. I asked Jill if Molly walked in a figure eight between her legs when she was a child. Jill was surprised to hear this—it was one of Molly's rituals. I also asked if she had a tickling feeling on her legs while sitting at her desk, as if she needs to brush something off her legs. Jill was momentarily quiet, as if surprised, and then validated she does have this feeling on her legs rather often. I informed Jill that this feeling on her legs was her childhood feline! Twenty years after Molly's death, Jill experiences Molly being near her in a special way. I could hear her voice change as she held back the tears. This kitty was close to her heart.

Molly also shared with me that Jill was hesitant to apply for a higher position within the business. Molly gave Jill encouragement, an extra boost, to reach for her dream. I do not know the results of Molly's encouragement. I do know Jill felt optimistic about her future, and now realizes loved ones who have passed over are with us.

28

Feet Walk

"If a man aspires toward a righteous life, his first act of abstinence is from injury to animals."

~Leo Tolstoy

Be "aware" of the wolf. Yet, dog will inhabit the earth, speaks a wise gray wolf dog named Delaware. Dog, known by man is the safer one; this is the way of man. And... forth came the dog to show man the way, yet man took dog and dominated him, and now dog lives in high rises. And...peace came to the dog to be with man to remind him of man's inner

134

self. And...more sidewalks man walked. And...now the gray one comes forth again to show the way. Listen to the howl of the dog wolves. Yes. They will show the way, for Wolf is different than dog, and looked upon differently, as man will soon look differently upon himself.

And...many wolf dogs have howled messages into the wind, delivering nature's way, the higher ways. Be at peace in your feet walk, be soft and gentle on your path. Life is filled with surprises, and to miss them would be akin to missing your higher guidance.

Forty-eight wolf dogs howled and barked in unison on a North Carolina mountainside. Time stood still. A dark night with few stars emphasized the symphony of a heavenly, resonating nature call. I heard it clearly: *Listen to your own nature call. Life is yours. Treasure each moment. Be one with all. Loving yourselves will help all of that which is called nature. Which is, also, you.*

Two rescued wolf dogs, Wolfie and Annie, ran with purpose to the edge of their wooded, fenced-in home at Full Moon Farm Inc, a rescue and sanctuary for abused and unwanted wolf dogs. Although I did not see them, I could feel their energy behind me as we walked away from their home to visit other wolf dogs. I turned to see them at the fence edge where I had been standing. Without hesitation, I walked back to the two wolf dogs and instinctively put my hand through the fence that separated us. Gently they licked my hand—soft, gentle, warm strokes. I had asked them earlier as we watched them keeping their distance, "If you have a message I will write it. Give me a sign." And they did.

Why has the spirit of the wolf drawn the attention of so many? I believe it is the call within ourselves wanting—needing—a better understanding of who we are and what we want on a deeper level. Wolves possess what we are looking for, and, therefore, we are attracted to them.

Ted Andrews gives us an understanding about wolves in his book *Animal - Speak*. "Their sense of family is strong and loyal, and they live by carefully defined rules and rituals.

Wolves do not fight unnecessarily. In fact, they will often go out of their way to avoid it. Wolf helps us to understand that true freedom requires discipline."

I suggest researching wolves to appreciate how they live in nature and apply it to your own "feet walk," as Delaware called it.

I found it interesting when Delaware said "dog wolfs." When humans speak of these mixed breeds, they say "wolf dogs" not "dog wolfs." I believe when Delaware was speaking of the dog wolf it was his way of saying, domesticated dog. The domesticated dog is a better companion for man than the wolf dog. Dog evolved from a wolf. A dog wolf that is more dog than wolf will bark, but ones with more wolf will howl. That night, I noticed all the wolf dogs began barking and howling at the same time and all ended at the same time. Whether more dog or wolf, they made their voices known as a group, as if all were one.

Nancy Brown, who heads Full Moon Farm, explained to me that Delaware was picked up without any ID in a state where wolf dogs are illegal to have as a pet. Only because he is such a sweetie was he saved, and only because one shelter worker went out of her way to find sanctuary for him is he alive. He was scheduled to die.

Delaware expressed that he missed children and wanted to go to schools. Nancy, who is telepathic with her animals, was preparing for an outreach program for first graders several weeks after my visit. She normally relied on Zodiac, another wolf dog at the sanctuary, yet when thinking about Zodiac she heard a loud voice in her head that said *NO! I want to go.* It was Delaware, who said to her, *You told the nice lady you would take ME to school.* He loved those kids so he was the perfect choice.

Delaware, Wolfie and Annie are extraordinary wolf dogs who have come to help us in our "feet walk," a term used by Delaware. Being in the presence of wolves brings a sense of freedom, wisdom, self-reliance, discipline, and harmony, qualities many people are looking for within themselves. To own a wolf dog does not give the person these qualities. To observe and understand the wolf, and then implement wolf's qualities into our own lives, can be profound.

After speaking with several of the wolf dogs at this sanctuary, I learned that some of them wanted to be free to live with the land and trees and to run where they wished. They would take responsibility for what might happen to them. These animals, however, most likely will never have the freedom of their ancestors.

We must be responsible with nature—with ourselves— who we are—what we do on a daily basis—a great message given to help us in our "feet walk."

~~~~~~~~~~~~•••~~~~~~~~~~~~

New Life

I am continually amazed by the gentleness of animal interactions with their people during sensitive times. Breyers was an emaciated little beagle who was hanging onto life for the sake of his person who could not yet let him go. Breyers had been with this woman for sixteen years. She wanted to be with her precious companion as long as possible, because Breyers had been there for her, giving unconditional love and companionship during difficult times. Yet, Breyers was now very sick. The tearful lady was pregnant and due for a C-section the next day. The sensitive, sweet beagle expressed to his person that he was going to give birth, too— to a new life—and that they should celebrate together with ice cream. How appropriate. Breyers passed the day after our communication.

Months later at an animal communication appearance, the parents of the lady who loved Breyers approached me. They were grateful for Breyers' wise words which helped their daughter and Breyers celebrate the life they had spent together, and the *new life* both were preparing to experience.
~~~~~~~~~~~~

How do I handle the emotions and upsets that are inevitably a part of animal communicating? I have come to realize that life contains many, many experiences. Without labeling them good or bad, I appreciate them all. I try to do my best when using my telepathic skills, and—mostly— listen from my heart for guidance.

29

Harmony and Height

"Man has great power of speech, but the greater part thereof is empty and deceitful. The animals have little, but that little is useful and true; and better is a small and certain thing than a great falsehood."

~Leonardo Da Vinci

Mesmerized, I watched as the eagle soared. No more than forty feet away, she flew over Smith Mountain Lake, the water glistening behind her. It was the only glimpse I had of her that spring, a gift that will be forever etched in my mind.

I was thrilled when Eagle appeared the following year. I found it interesting that she presented herself in the same location, at water's edge in front of our home, yet this time she flew in from the opposite direction. She was beautiful. Eagle showed herself again a few days later while my husband, John, and I were canoeing. My eyes were drawn to her perch on the tallest tree.

I sensed she had a message.

Our thoughts intertwined. *Tomorrow,* she told me, *before the sun is high in the sky; later I will be resting.*

However, a two-way communication did not immediately take place. I was receiving information from Eagle, but it was coming too fast, all at one time, like a book in front of my face that I was required to read in one second. I became frustrated and decided I would try to communicate again later on.

The situation took an interesting turn a few days later.

Over and over I heard a voice in my head guiding me to go on the Internet to research bald eagles. I am uncertain if these words were the eagle's or perhaps my own higher guidance. Which ever one it was, I have learned to honor the guidance that comes to me in this manner. I was anxious to see what information I would find.

As I began my research, I was guided directly to Eagle's message.

My Internet search for bald eagle quickly took me to "The Great Seal of the United States—A Message from America's Founders." I felt a chill run down my spine when I read the title: "The Eagle Speaks." Here on the Web, historian John D. MacArthur explains the symbolism of the Great Seal taken from the Franklin Institute Science Museum's website, published in 1998,

While I read, I knew in my heart that the message so eloquently written by John MacArthur was also my Eagle's message, one I could not fully comprehend on my own. With MacArthur's permission, I have printed the following information, with respect to the great American Bald Eagle.

The Eagle Speaks

I landed on that peculiar paper you call money during the Civil War and on the back of your dollar during the World War. Since 1935 I have shared the greenback with the pyramid and eye whose keen vision, like mine, bridges Heaven and Earth.

For those who say I represent power and might, I tell you that is not me. I am more of harmony and height, soaring spirit and simple joys. Yes, I have strength, but it is so I can nourish my children nested high in the hallowed arms of Earth.

Let me be for you a living reminder, a messenger of Unity from the ancestors of this land, and for all who would transform the red dust into the sacred circle. This is the meaning of the Latin words on the scroll I carry, E Pluribus Unum— Out of Many, One.

You are one with your ancestors, one with your descendents, one with the creatures of land, sky, and water—even with the rooted ones. Remember this, and your heart will soar with the spirit of the Eagle.

In addition, I learned that the Great Seal of the United States has two sides. The American Bald Eagle graces one side; a symbolic great pyramid is dedicated on the other side.

I wondered if I would see Eagle again. I wanted to take a picture of her to possibly use in my book. Then, quite suddenly, another message came from Eagle: *The treasured picture will be of the Great American Bald Eagle seal.* I realized then that the "treasured" picture Eagle referred to was not the one I would take with my camera, but the picture of the Great American Bald Eagle Seal. I assumed she referred to the American Bald Eagle side, not the Great Pyramid side. That is how I made sense of her message at that time.

Several months after I received this message, I again contacted John MacArthur. He told me of a new seal he had created, imposing the American Bald Eagle on the Great Pyramid. He calls it the "Seal of United America." It reflects the American Eagle's call for unity—"E pluribus Unum"— Out of Many, One. When Eagle said, "The treasured picture will be of the great American Bald Eagle seal," was she speaking of MacArthur's new seal?

Eagle pushed me to think about my values, beliefs, and my responsibilities. Do we "treasure" our country as much as our forefathers did? Have we governed our country in the way our forefathers intended? In these times, are we "united" with our country, families, communities, or God? Are we, on a personal level, united with ourselves—are we honoring, loving, and respecting ourselves?

I asked Eagle how to end this message. She answered: *There is no end. It continues forever.* I recalled the following statement by John F. Kennedy. I could not ignore his message:

"American history is not something dead and over. It is always alive, always growing, always unfinished—and every American today has his own contribution to make to the great fabric of tradition and hope which binds all Americans, dead and living and yet to be born, in a common faith and a common destiny."

There is no end, it continues forever.

Eagle knows this, I am convinced she is using me to pass this on.

For more information on the Great Seal, go to www. GreatSeal.com.

30

Nuts and Bolts of an
Animal Communication

"If you talk to the animals, they will talk with you and you will know each other. If you do not talk to them, you will not know them, and what you do not know, you will fear. What one fears, one destroys."

~Chief Dan George

How I receive and give information from the nature kingdom has been predominately a self-learned process. My explanations and examples, therefore, may be different from other animal communicators. I recommend to those wanting to learn animal communication to take classes or read books from different communicators. The wider the variety of personalities in teachers and their techniques the more you will learn.

Although I had communicated naturally with animals all of my life, I wanted to learn more. I attended two classes and read three books on the subject. My efforts helped me understand what I was doing instinctively and gave me techniques to enhance my communications.

For me, one of the most difficult parts in becoming a communicator was learning to express precisely what I received from the animals. I understood the messages from the animal, yet translating the information accurately so that the client understood the information as clearly as I did, at times, was a challenge. I may use several words or sentences to describe one feeling or simple bit of information for clarity.

High emotions concerning a person's animal can bring a state of mind that affects the personality to hear correctly. If I sense my client did not understand what I communicated to her, I ask her to explain back to me, in her words, what I said to her. I do this to make certain my client is correctly receiving what I am conveying.

Reasons for a Communication

Think out of the box for reasons why people would call for a communication. A few unusual reasons are: Tell Maggie she has to live for at least five more years. You must tell my horse he has to do everything I want him to do whenever I want him to do it. Tell my dog he can not pee or poop for ten hours. He must wait until I get home from work. Obviously, not all requests are resolved the way the person prefers. My more common communications are about urinating in unwanted places, fear-based issues, clawing, barking, lost, and sick animals and dominance over people, toys, and food. Many communications evolve around their critter needing a better diet, more exercise and mental stimulation. I provide support for the animal and person; before, during, after the death of an animal, plus messages from the animal once he has passed over. I also help pets handle changes with home, job, relationships, travel, and moving, providing conversation between the animal and his person as friends would.

Phone communications are not limited to one individual. Pony clubs, couples, mothers and their children can engage with the use of a speaker phone. I do not limit my communications to one animal per session.

Animals can be witty, serious, nonchalant, funny, bold, and sometimes what we humans would call rude. To understand these behaviors I look at the people and circumstances that have affected their lives. For example: the personality of a loving, patient young horse changed to a bit bossy and indignant after staying with a trainer for several months. I discovered the trainer had the same personality.

When the animal gives me sensitive information, I share a small portion of this information with the person and then ask for permission to continue. So far, everyone has wanted to continue. This part of the communication often surprises people I am working with for the first time. I usually hear my client say, *I had no idea my animal was so wise or I knew she was smart, but I could not understand what she was trying to tell me.*

Prior to the Communication

The communication begins with a phone call. Behind a concerned, frightened or over-anxious voice I hear a brief explanation as to why the client wants a communication. I then explain to them how to best work with me so that they can have a good communication.

First, we set an appointment. In an emergency, as in: lost, extremely ill, or if an animal is close to passing over, I will give the communication as soon as possible.

Next, I give the client "homework," to write a list of detailed questions for his animal or animals. Homework fine-tunes the original purpose for a communication and can usually help the person think of other needs to be addressed. I have had from three to thirty questions listed for one session. The number of questions is not always relevant to how long the communication lasts. Many times one statement from the animal can answer several questions. On the other hand, the answer to one question could last half of an hour.

I emphasize to my clients the importance of being in a comfortable, relaxed place where they will not be interrupted. I believe this state of mind and body helps the flow of information among all of us, and clients are more likely to understand and add to the quality of the communication.

I have found memory sometimes fails after a communication. I suggest the client have a pad of paper and pen to write down important information. Writing the details revealed in a communication also helps clients retain the messages correctly, even if they do not revisit their notes. I also take notes during and after the communication to re-examine before their next communication. I do not record my communications at this time because I travel, staying in hotel rooms, visiting homes, and, in cases of emergencies, I have communicated in the middle of a hardware store, convention center, sitting on top of a stone wall in Savannah, Georgia and even on a sail boat on the Intercostal Waterway.

Many clients prefer their animal to be near them during the session. I explain that the animal or animals we are communicating with can be wherever they want. I consider their comfort and needs as well as my human clients. Frequently the animal also wants to be close during the session. A popular place people like to have a communication is on their bed, relaxed with critters around them. Horse owners like to be near or in the stall. The extreme opposite is when the animal and person are on different sides of the planet. These communications are as successful as those side by side.

Unusual animal behavior during a communication adds to the experience. Once when a cat and I thought we were finished, the cat walked out of the room. Another cat in the household was ready to communicate and he walked into the room. Then the cats' person unexpectedly had another question for the first cat. The first cat did an about-face at that moment and walked back into the room, as the second cat walked out. Most often the pet stares into their person's eyes or gives physical gestures using their paws to pat the leg or face or a wet lick when giving important information. And some animals immediately fall asleep as the session begins.

I ask the client if we need to keep our session to a specific time frame, or if they would like an open-ended session.

If I sense my client has intuitive abilities, I offer teaching animal communication in their session. My offer is often eagerly accepted unless the communication focus is too emotional. I inform the client their communication/teaching session will last longer than when I alone give the communication.

I ask my client to call me at the time of the appointment. I find when the client takes on the responsibility to call me at our appointment time, they are better prepared, and on time.

Before the communication begins, I explain that when I am quiet I am receiving information or discerning how best to express information I have received. When there is silence in a phone conversation it is normal to feel the need to talk. I let the client know at these times that honoring the silence makes for a better communication.

I ask my client to please let me know if I share any information that he does not understand, or that appears incorrect. I can then revisit the information to see if I misinterpreted, or need more information to better comprehend. There have been times when the person questions the information I receive, however, I have to hold true to my information. Usually, later in the communication, or even days later, the puzzling information is clarified.

I was in a communication with a cat that had passed over. He told me that he was with the blue baby. At the time, my client did not understand this information. A few weeks later she emailed saying her mother-in-law had lost a baby at birth. The baby had turned blue.

Telepathy, How I Receive Information

How do I get information from the animals? I like the simple dictionary explanation for telepathy: it is "the transfer of thoughts and images from one being to another." I liken this information transfer to a TV station sending a transmission to our TVs. One tunes into the channel she wants or in my case, I tune into or focus on the animal I want.

With a quiet, calm mind and body, I maintain a spacious open awareness. Pictures, words, emotions, as well as symbols, smells, sounds and tastes come to me. My body can feel what the animal's body feels—pain, cramps or stiffness. Usually, several of the above senses take place in one communication.

I step out of my personal belief system. I maintain an open, unrestricted state of mind with unconditional love focused on the animal and the person I am working with. Doing this creates awareness beyond the analytical mind. At times it feels as if I made up the information I received, yet this feeling also tells me the thoughts did not come from me. Knowing the difference between thoughts that feel like your own, from those that are from animal thoughts takes practice. Some might believe it is their imagination at work and want to discard what they are experiencing, yet it is from our imagination that we find the answers. As Albert Einstein said, "Imagination is more important than knowledge."

The Communication Begins

I begin our session asking for basic information—age, breed, and color, how and where the animal came into my client's life, and how long the person has been with the animal. I then write her questions in my note book which gives me a preview of what the person wants out of the communication and how my client perceives her animal's behavior. Knowing all of the questions also gives me an opportunity to intuit and better understand the bigger picture of what is going on between the animal and person.

Often, several questions concerning what appears to be different behaviors are one issue. Taffy is hyper, plays catch-me-if-you-can and runs away from home when she has the opportunity. Three different issues are addressed with one answer. In this particular case, Taffy, a young dog, needed more exercise and training.

On the flip side, what appears to be the same behavior has different causes for the behavior. Spot barks at his person unpredictably when he is working at the computer. Spot sees his person has been working too long and needs a break. Spot knows his person needs to take his medication. Spot needs to go outside. All three answers pertain to the same action from Spot.

One of the biggest concerns I hear is, how do I know I am communicating with the correct animal? This is a good question, because 95% of my communications are on the phone. Sometimes, I have a picture to work from. Typically, I see in my mind's eye a specific marking on the animal's body his person can validate. For example: I see a picture in my mind of a back right leg that is white up to the elbow. I usually do not see the whole body, just what I need to see to validate I have the correct critter. I find it interesting that some people have to look at their animal to see if what I said is true and then notice a marking that they did not notice before. A cat, Tuxedo Boy, had a couple of white hairs nestled into the tip of his tail. His people had no idea they were there.

When I telepathically tune into the animal I never quite know what to expect. The animal usually has her own agenda before we address the person's questions, although inadvertently some of the questions are answered.

The first few words or sentences can be extremely important. This statement is usually a simple answer concerning the core purpose for the communication. Animals are simple minded. People are not. We need details to help us understand; animals simply know.

A dog's opening statement to his person, was "My person is overly stressed." He told her to "chill out!" The dog preceded with suggestions for his person to help change her belief system and actions that caused her stressed life. The outcome was a person and dog with less stress. Animals react from their person's stress or any mood. A bad dog, so perceived by his person, turned into a good dog, not leaving his poop on the carpet.

The first words in a communication with Little Miss Kitty were, "You worry too much." I was amazed as I observed an involved unraveling of how worry created a depressed life. These emotions affected Kitty who was now peeing outside of the litter box and hiding under the bed. Little Miss Kitty's person was now focused on managing, and/or letting go of her worries and taking personal time to rediscover what makes her happy—as simple as what ice cream she likes best. As the communication winds down, usually the critter expresses her original or a similar statement again, which brings the communication full circle. Kitty also put a request in for a high seat at their sunroom window to watch the birds and other animals—a good example of knowing what one enjoys.

Ending the Communication

As the communication comes to an end, I feel the energy of the animal backing off. All questions have been addressed. I ask the person if he feels complete with the session. Usually he does, yet I sense a searching of the brain for hidden questions. Sometimes I am the one who does not feel complete and will focus back to the animal or situation being addressed for more insights.

After a session with clients who have been given a lot of information, particularly insights into their own life, I suggest they take some quiet time to process what the communication gave them. An example: the person admits there is abuse in his life and the animal is acting out because of it.

Most communications end with happy, contented feelings. For instance, a person has a better understanding of her fearful animal and the animal now understands his fearful behavior no longer supports his survival. Sadie is another example; she is a mischievous dog when her people are on vacation. Sadie expressed she wanted to stay with Aunt Mary instead of the neighbors while her people are gone. This simple change alleviated the problem.

Clients often ask if the animals contact me when I am not in a session. Yes, they do. I may receive details from the animal, or I keep thinking of the animals' persons until I finally realize I should call them. I then hear, "I have been meaning to call to set an appointment," or I will ask how they and their critter are doing, and usually there is a situation that needs to be addressed. I have also found my client may call me when they come to my mind. It feels like trying to figure out which came first, the chicken or the egg. Most likely, both of us are picking up on the animal's energy and/or each other. It simply becomes a matter of who makes the effort to call first.

I advise my clients to discern the information given to them. Think about it in different ways or views. Most likely, they will understand and retrieve more information yet. Some information they may want to toss, and some put in their back pocket for future understanding or use.

I end the communication by thanking all parties for allowing me to communicate with them. If it is not verbally spoken, I send the energy or emotion of being thankful.

I am grateful that I have wonderful clients. Many are now friends. I cherish each and every one, and the critters that brought us together.

Afterword

When I met Karen, I was in a state of depression, high stress, and low self-esteem. This emotional state manifested itself in many physical ailments as well as family dynamics which were tense, angry, and fearful. Karen helped me to see that my dogs feel and reflect my emotions. "Animals are a mirror to our soul." This is one of many profound realizations I have made after working with Karen Wrigley.

For the past year Karen has taught me to communicate telepathically with my dogs by combining her energy with mine in joint communications with my dogs. In these joint communications, Karen teaches me simple techniques to allow myself to receive communications, as well as different ways to elicit answers to questions I want answered. At first, it was painfully difficult. I was only able to receive simple yes/no answers. Karen would then provide the more detailed interpretation of the communication. When she provided this information, it validated my own communication and also helped me to understand what I had received. In addition, Karen taught me to keep asking questions in order to be specifically clear to the animal exactly what it was I was asking so that the answer was understood and answered correctly. During these ongoing communications, each of my dogs exhibits his or her own unique personality, wit, and sense of humor. As time progressed, I started to receive clear images, single words, strong emotions (elation and grief), as well as flashes of complete understanding. These communications from my pets and other animals help me to understand their wants and needs. The most common time for my animals to communicate unsolicited information to me is when I am totally relaxed (in the hot shower, drifting off to sleep, and brushing my teeth are examples of the most frequent occurrences).

I have come to understand most animals are connected directly to the universe in a beautiful, spiritual way, and thus are able to provide us with amazing wisdom beyond anything I ever thought an animal or even a human was capable of! This is the part of animal communications that was the big surprise to me.

Communicating with animals is not simply about finding out what their favorite toy is, or whether they are hungry or not. There is a deeper, more spiritual aspect. Animals are directly tuned into the universal plan. Their wisdom is directly channeled from the universe itself. They are messengers from God. They understand and tell us things that they cannot possibly fabricate within their own minds. This wisdom is so cosmic, so beautiful, and so inspiring that I have regained hope for mankind and for the universe. There is no other explanation for how a bird can impart such universal wisdom to us via animal communicators such as Karen. They and we are merely a conduit for messages from the universe itself.

—Carol

Illustrations with quotes and book cover picture
are available in various items through my website at
www.karenwrigley.com

Notes

Notes